UNDERGROUND CLINICAL VIGNE...

BIOCHEMISTRY

Classic Clinical Cases
for USMLE Step 1 & 2 Review [101 cases, 1st ed]

VIKAS BHUSHAN, MD
University of California, San Francisco, Class of 1991
Series Editor, Diagnostic Radiologist

CHIRAG AMIN, MD
University of Miami, Class of 1996
Orlando Regional Medical Center, Resident in Orthopaedic Surgery

TAO LE, MD
University of California, San Francisco, Class of 1996
Yale-New Haven Hospital, Resident in Internal Medicine

JOSE M. FIERRO, MD
La Salle University, Mexico City
Brookdale University Hospital, New York, Intern in Medicine/Pediatrics

VISHAL PALL, MBBS
Government Medical College, Chandigarh, India, Class of 1996

HOANG NGUYEN
Northwestern University, Medical Scientist Training Program

Cover Design: Ashley Pound

Editor: Andrea Fellows

This book was created with MS Word97 using the following typefaces: Garamond, Futura Medium, and Futura ExtraBold. The cases were developed in a master table and converted into pages by a macro written by Alex Grimm. The camera-ready copy was created on a Lexmark Optra R by Vikas Bhushan.

Printed in the USA

ISBN: 1-890061-08-5

Contributors

SAMIR MEHTA
Temple University, Class of 2000

ALEA EUSEBIO
UCLA School of Medicine, Class of 2000

VIPAL SONI
UCLA School of Medicine, Class of 1999

Acknowledgments

Throughout the production of this book, we have had the support of many friends and colleagues. Special thanks to our administrative assistant, Gianni Le Nguyen. For expert computer support, Tarun Mathur (hardware) and Alex Grimm (software). For editing, proofreading, and assistance, thanks to Cecilia Wieslander and Ken Lin.

Table of Contents

Case	Subspecialty	Name
42	Endocrinology	Vitamin A Deficiency
43	Endocrinology	Vitamin K Deficiency
44	Gastroenterology	Antabuse Effect
45	Gastroenterology	Carcinoid Syndrome
46	Gastroenterology	Crigler–Najjar Syndrome
47	Gastroenterology	Dubin–Johnson Syndrome
48	Gastroenterology	Gilbert's Disease
49	Genetics	Acute Intermittent Porphyria
50	Genetics	Albinism
51	Genetics	Alkaptonuria
52	Genetics	Chronic Granulomatous Disease
53	Genetics	Cystic Fibrosis
54	Genetics	Cystinuria
55	Genetics	Duchenne's Muscular Dystrophy
56	Genetics	Ehlers–Danlos Syndrome
57	Genetics	Fabry's Disease
58	Genetics	Familial Hyper-cholesterolemia
59	Genetics	Familial Hypertriglyceridemia
60	Genetics	Fanconi's Anemia
61	Genetics	Fragile X Syndrome
62	Genetics	Galactosemia
63	Genetics	Gaucher's Disease
64	Genetics	Hereditary Fructose Intolerance
65	Genetics	Homocystinuria
66	Genetics	Hunter's Disease
67	Genetics	Hurler's disease
68	Genetics	Kartagener's Syndrome
69	Genetics	Krabbe's Disease
70	Genetics	Lesch–Nyhan Syndrome
71	Genetics	Maple Syrup Urine Disease
72	Genetics	Metachromatic Leukodystrophy
73	Genetics	Niemann–Pick Disease
74	Genetics	Orotic Aciduria
75	Genetics	Osteogenesis Imperfecta
76	Genetics	Paroxysmal Nocturnal Hemoglobinuria
77	Genetics	Phenylketonuria (PKU)
78	Genetics	Phosphoenolpyruvate Carboxykinase
79	Genetics	Pompe's Disease
80	Genetics	Pyruvate Kinase Deficiency
81	Genetics	Tay–Sachs Disease
82	Genetics	von Gierke's Disease
83	Genetics	Wilson's Disease
84	Genetics	Xeroderma Pigmentosum
85	Heme/Onc	Folate Deficiency
86	Heme/Onc	Glucose-6-Phosphate Dehydrogenase
87	Heme/Onc	Hemophilia

Case	Subspecialty	Name
88	Heme/Onc	Hereditary Spherocytosis
89	Heme/Onc	Iron-Deficiency Anemia
90	Heme/Onc	Methemoglobinemia
91	Heme/Onc	Pernicious Anemia
92	Heme/Onc	Porphyria Cutanea Tarda
93	Heme/Onc	Rhabdomyolysis
94	Heme/Onc	Sickle Cell Anemia
95	Heme/Onc	Thalassemia
96	Heme/Onc	von Willebrand's Disease
97	Pulmonary	Acute Respiratory Distress Syndrome
98	Pulmonary	Alpha-1-Antitrypsin Deficiency
99	Pulmonary	Anxiety Hyperventilation
100	Pulmonary	Carbon Monoxide Narcosis
101	Pulmonary	Hyaline Membrane Disease

Preface

This series was developed to address the increasing number of clinical vignette questions on the USMLE Step 1 and Step 2. It is designed to supplement and complement *First Aid for the USMLE Step 1* (Appleton & Lange).

Each book uses a series of approximately 100 **"supra-prototypical" cases as a way to condense testable facts and associations**. The clinical vignettes in this series are designed to incorporate as many testable facts as possible into a cohesive and memorable clinical picture. The vignettes represent composites drawn from general and specialty textbooks, reference books, thousands of USMLE style questions and the personal experience of the authors and reviewers.

Although each case tends to present all the signs, symptoms, and diagnostic findings for a particular illness, **patients generally will not present with such a "complete" picture either clinically or on the Step 1 exam**. Cases are not meant to simulate a potential real patient or an exam vignette. All the **boldfaced "buzzwords" are for learning purposes** and are not necessarily expected to be found in any one patient with the disease.

Definitions of selected important terms are placed within the vignettes in (= SMALL CAPS) in parentheses. Other parenthetical remarks often refer to the pathophysiology or mechanism of disease. The format should also help students learn to present cases succinctly during oral "bullet" presentations on clinical rotations. The cases are meant to be read as a condensed review, not as a primary reference.

The information provided in this book has been prepared with a great deal of thought and careful research. This book should not, however, be considered as your sole source of information. Corrections, suggestions and submissions of new cases are encouraged and will be acknowledged and incorporated in future editions (see How to Contribute).

How to Contribute

We invite your corrections and suggestions for the next edition of this book. **For the first submission of each factual correction or new vignette, you will receive a personal acknowledgment and a free copy of the revised book.**

We prefer that you submit corrections or suggestions via electronic mail to **vbhushan@aol.com**. Please include "Underground Vignettes" as the subject of your message.

For corrections to this book, visit our Student to Student Medical Publishing Site at:

http://www.s2smed.com

If you do not have access to e-mail, use the following mailing address: S2S Medical Publishing, 1015 Gayley Ave, Box 1113, Los Angeles, CA 90024 USA.

Abbreviations

ID/CC	identification and chief complaint
HPI	history of present illness
PE	physical exam

ABGs	arterial blood gases
CBC	complete blood count
ECG	electrocardiography
EMG	electromyography
LYTES	electrolytes
PBS	peripheral blood smear
PE	physical exam
PFTs	pulmonary function tests
UA	urinalysis
VS	vital signs

Angio	angiography
BE	barium enema
CT	computerized tomography
CXR	chest x-ray
Echo	echocardiography
EEG	electroencephalography
EGD	esophagogastroduodenoscopy
ERCP	endoscopic retrograde cholangiopancreatography
FNA	fine needle aspiration
HIDA	hepatoiminodiacetic acid [scan]
IVP	intravenous pyelography
KUB	kidneys/ureter/bladder
LP	lumbar puncture
Mammo	mammography
MR	magnetic resonance [imaging]
Nuc	nuclear medicine
PA	posteroanterior
PET	positron emission tomography
SBFT	small bowel follow through [barium study]
UGI	upper GI [barium study]
US	ultrasound
V/Q	ventilation perfusion
XR	x-ray

1 17-Alpha-Hydroxylase Deficiency

ID/CC A 16-year-old girl is referred to an endocrinologist due to **lack of menses** (= AMENORRHEA) and absence of pubic hair, axillary hair, and breast development (= LACK OF SECONDARY SEXUAL CHARACTERISTICS).

HPI She also complains of frequent **headaches and ringing in her ears** (due to hypertension).

PE VS: hypertension (BP 160/105). PE: funduscopic exam normal; no lymphadenopathy; no hepatosplenomegaly; absence of breast tissue; no abdominal or pelvic masses palpable; no axillary or pubic hair; vulvar labia normal.

Labs Lytes: low blood potassium levels (= HYPOKALEMIA); increased sodium levels (= HYPERNATREMIA). ABGs: metabolic alkalosis (due to mineralocorticoid action of 11-deoxycorticosterone and corticosterone). Suppressed renin; increase in urinary gonadotropins (due to attempt to compensate for lack of sex hormones); diminished 17-ketosteroids (product of sex hormones).

Imaging N/A

Gross Pathology N/A

Micro Pathology N/A

Treatment Glucocorticoids. Sex hormones.

Discussion Decrease in 17-alpha-hydroxylase produces an increase in 11-deoxycorticosterone and corticosterone (due to shifting of metabolism from sex hormones to aldosterone pathway); renin suppressed (due to aldosterone negative feedback). Females fail to develop secondary sexual characteristics; males develop ambiguous external genitalia (= MALE PSEUDOHERMAPHRODITISM).

21-Hydroxylase Deficiency

ID/CC   A newborn is evaluated by a neonatologist because the intern who performed the delivery **cannot tell whether the child is male or female** (= AMBIGUOUS GENITALIA).

HPI   The child is also **lethargic** and lacks sufficient strength to suck on mother's milk adequately (due to salt wasting).

PE   Ambiguous external genitalia; **increase in size of clitoris; fusion of labia** to the point of resembling scrotal sac.

Labs   Lytes: **low blood sodium** (= HYPONATREMIA); **elevated blood potassium** (= HYPERKALEMIA). **Increase in 17-alpha-OH progesterone** and its metabolite, **pregnanetriol; increase in urinary 17-ketosteroids** (defect is distal to 17, 20-desmolase); elevated serum adrenalcorticotropic hormone (= ACTH). Prenatal diagnosis possible at 14–16 weeks (due to increase in 17-alpha-OH progesterone).

Imaging   N/A

Gross Pathology   N/A

Micro Pathology   N/A

Treatment   Cortisol, dehydrocorticosterone acetate if salt wasting is present.

Discussion   Most common form of congenital adrenal hyperplasia. Lack of 21-hydroxylase causes a decrease in cortisol with a consequent increase in ACTH, which in turn produces hyperplasia of adrenals and a resulting increase in androgen production, giving rise to signs of female pseudohermaphroditism (as in this case) and enlarged genitalia in the male. May occur with or without salt wasting.

5-Alpha-Reductase Deficiency

ID/CC   A 5-year-old boy is brought to the pediatrician by his father, who recently discovered that his son **does not urinate through his penis.**

HPI   The patient's father also reports that he cannot find his son's testes (due to cryptorchidism).

PE   Penis small for age (= MICROPHALLIA); testes located in inguinal canal bilaterally (= CRYPTORCHIDISM); urinary meatus lies in perineum (= HYPOSPADIAS); scrotal sac bifid.

Labs   **Markedly reduced 5-alpha-dihydrotestosterone with normal testosterone level.**

Imaging   N/A

Gross Pathology   N/A

Micro Pathology   N/A

Treatment   Dihydrotestosterone.

Discussion   Autosomal-recessive disorder of virilization. Lack of 5-alpha-reductase produces a decrease in 5-alpha-dihydrotestosterone, which is responsible for virilization of external genitalia.

ID/CC	A 43-year-old white male comes to the emergency room complaining of severe retroorbital **headache** (behind his eyes) along with **blurred vision**.
HPI	He also complains of weakness over the past few months and acknowledges an **increase in hat size** as well as an inability to wear his wedding ring (due to growth in finger width). His family also notes a **coarsening of his facial features and deepening of his voice**.
PE	VS: hypertension (BP 150/100). PE: skin thick and oily; **prominent forehead and jaw;** enlarged tongue and widening gaps between teeth; **large hands and feet; bitemporal hemianopsia;** cardiomegaly; hepatosplenomegaly.
Labs	**Hyperglycemia;** hyperphosphatemia; **increased levels of growth hormone** (GH) and prolactin.
Imaging	XR: thickening of skull; erosion and **enlargement of sella turcica;** widening distal phalanges in hands and feet. MR - Head: enlarged pituitary gland containing a mass.
Gross Pathology	Acidophilic adenoma of pituitary gland with ill-defined capsule exerts mass effects on pituitary and nearby optic chiasm; tumor rarely malignant.
Micro Pathology	Densely packed, mature cells that are highly granulocytic and eosinophilic; stain highly for GH.
Treatment	Hypophysectomy (transsphenoidal approach) with subsequent hormone replacement.
Discussion	Most common cause is pituitary adenoma. If excess GH secretion is present in **childhood, gigantism** appears; **in adults, acromegaly.** Headache and joint pain are early complaints; blurred vision and visual-field changes occur later. Almost every organ in the body increases in size. 25% exhibit glucose intolerance. Visual field changes (e.g., bitemporal hemianopsia) may occur secondary to compression of the nerves of the optic chiasm by the tumor.

ID/CC A 37-year-old female is admitted to the internal medicine ward for evaluation of **increasing weakness** and intermittent episodes of **dizziness, nausea, and vomiting** that are **related to stress and exercise.**

HPI She is a vegetarian, takes no drugs or medications, and does not drink alcohol or smoke cigarettes. She reports an excessive **craving for salty foods** such as chips and salted peanuts.

PE VS: **tachycardia** (110); **hypotension** (BP 90/65). PE: patient thin with dry mucous membranes; **pigmentation of buccal mucosa and palms of hands;** no neck masses; chest auscultation normal; no abdominal masses; no hepatosplenomegaly; no lymphadenopathy.

Labs CBC: normal. Lytes: **hyponatremia; hyperkalemia. Glucose low; increased blood urea nitrogen (BUN) with normal creatinine;** amylase and liver function tests normal; **high adrenocorticotropic hormone (ACTH); low cortisol.**

Imaging N/A

Gross Pathology N/A

Micro Pathology N/A

Treatment Glucocorticoid and mineralocorticoid hormones. Hydrocortisone on an emergent basis.

Discussion Primary hypoadrenalism (= ADDISON'S DISEASE) may be caused by autoimmune mechanisms, tuberculous infection, or sudden discontinuation of chronic steroid administration. Secondary hypoadrenalism is due to abnormalities of hypothalamic-pituitary function.

ID/CC   A **15-year-old** female is admitted to the hospital for evaluation of persistent **weakness** for the last six months that has been unresponsive to multivitamin treatment.

HPI   She denies allergies, surgeries, psychological problems, transfusions, drug use, or any relevant past medical history.

PE   VS: heart rate normal; no fever; **hypertension** (BP 120/70) (excludes primary hyperaldosteronism). PE: patient well hydrated; pupils equal and reactive to light and accommodation; no neck masses; no lymphadenopathy; chest normal; abdomen soft and nontender; no masses; neurologic exam normal; **no peripheral edema;** sexual development appropriate to age.

Labs   CBC: normal. Lytes: **hyponatremia; hypokalemia. ABGs: metabolic alkalosis. Increased plasma renin** (excludes primary hyperaldosteronism); increased urinary excretion of prostaglandins.

Imaging   N/A

Gross Pathology   N/A

Micro Pathology   **Juxtaglomerular cell hyperplasia** on renal biopsy.

Treatment   Indomethacin to decrease prostaglandin synthesis.

Discussion   A type of secondary hyperaldosteronism in which there is an intrarenal defect in the reabsorptive conservation mechanism of sodium (due to resistance to angiotensin), with urinary sodium wasting and a consequent increase in renin production (through increased renal prostaglandins) and thus an increase in aldosterone activity with hypokalemic alkalosis. The hypokalemia perpetuates the cycle by stimulating renin activity.

7 Beriberi (Vitamin B1 Deficiency)

ID/CC   A 36-year-old black male who is known to be an **alcoholic** comes to the emergency room with shortness of breath, confusion, **foot drop,** and swelling of his legs.

HPI   He admits to getting drunk at least three times a week. His **diet** consists mainly of canned soup and cheap "junk food" that he eats during the periods in which he is not drunk.

PE   VS: tachycardia. PE: dyspnea; jugular venous distention; **extremities warm** to touch; cardiomegaly; hepatomegaly; 2+ pitting edema of both lower extremities; confusion with **nystagmus;** decreased deep tendon reflexes.

Labs   Low transketolase levels in erythrocytes.

Imaging   CXR: cardiomegaly with basal lung congestion.

Gross Pathology   Wernicke–Korsakoff encephalopathy shows congestion, hemorrhages, and necrosis in thalamus, hypothalamus (mammillary bodies), and paraventricular regions.

Micro Pathology   Demyelinization of peripheral nerves with axonal degeneration and fragmentation.

Treatment   Thiamine. Before administering glucose to an alcoholic, thiamine should be given to prevent encephalopathy. Alcoholics should also receive IV or oral folate and multivitamins.

Discussion   Lack of thiamine produces Wernicke–Korsakoff syndrome as well as **high-output heart failure (wet beriberi) and polyneuropathy (dry beriberi).** Thiamine pyrophosphate (TPP) is a cofactor for the Krebs cycle enzymes alpha-ketoglutarate dehydrogenase and pyruvate dehydrogenase as well as transketolase (pentose phosphate pathway).

ID/CC	A 39-year-old woman is referred to an internist by her family practitioner because of persistent **hypertension** that has been **unresponsive to conventional treatment;** she also complains of profound **muscle weakness** (due to hypokalemia).
HPI	She is a two-pack-a-day smoker and drinks occasionally.
PE	VS: normal heart rate; **hypertension** (BP 200/100). PE: no pallor; **retinal hemorrhages, exudates, and A-V nicking;** lungs clear; no heart murmurs; abdomen soft; no palpable masses; no lymphadenopathy.
Labs	CBC: increased hematocrit. Lytes: **hypokalemia; hypernatremia** (secondary to hyperaldosteronism). ABGs: **high serum bicarbonate.** Glucose normal (vs. ectopic ACTH production). ECG: left ventricular hypertrophy and strain. UA: no proteinuria. **Aldosterone levels high; renin levels low** (primary hyperaldosteronism).
Imaging	CT/MR: 1.7-cm enhancing left adrenal mass.
Gross Pathology	N/A
Micro Pathology	Glomerulosa-cell benign adrenal adenoma.
Treatment	Left adrenalectomy.
Discussion	Primary hyperaldosteronism typically presents with hypertension, hypokalemia, hypernatremia, and increased bicarbonate due to increased secretion of aldosterone by an adrenal adenoma (Conn's syndrome) or hyperplasia. Hypertension is characteristically **unresponsive to ACE** (= ANGIOTENSIN CONVERTING ENZYME) **inhibitors.** Surgically correctable causes of hypertension include Conn's syndrome, pheochromocytoma, renal artery stenosis, and coarctation of the aorta.

ID/CC   A 1-year-old female is taken to the emergency room because of **persistent vomiting** (20 times in 24 hours) that has been unresponsive to intramuscular antiemetics.

HPI   While on a family vacation to Florida, she was given vanilla ice cream that was being sold on the street (dairy and meat products may harbor staphylococcal enterotoxins that produce food poisoning).

PE   VS: tachycardia; mild fever; hypotension. PE. low urinary volume; **eyes sunken; poor skin turgor** with dryness of skin and mucous membranes; **lethargy and proximal muscle weakness** (due to hypokalemia); contraction of facial muscles upon tapping facial nerve anterior to ear (= POSITIVE CHVOSTEK'S SIGN); carpal spasm after occlusion of brachial artery with BP cuff (= TROUSSEAU'S SIGN) (hypocalcemia and metabolic alkalosis due to loss of hydrochloric acid).

Labs   CBC: increased hematocrit (due to hemoconcentration); increased blood urea nitrogen (BUN). Lytes: **hypokalemia;** hypochloremia. Hypocalcemia. UA: proteinuria; **high specific gravity.** ABGs: **metabolic alkalosis.** ECG: S-T-segment and T-wave depression; U waves (hypokalemia).

Imaging   N/A

Gross Pathology   N/A

Micro Pathology   N/A

Treatment   Fluid and electrolyte replacement.

Discussion   Dehydration may be isotonic, hypotonic, or hypertonic. When caused by protracted vomiting, it leads to metabolic alkalosis due to a decrease in hydrogen ion concentration with a compensatory rise in PCO_2 (due to diminished alveolar ventilation). The contraction of volume will stimulate the proximal renal tubular cells to reabsorb bicarbonate in spite of alkalosis.

ID/CC   A 27-year-old white male complains of **excessive thirst** (= POLYDIPSIA) and **increased urination** (= POLYURIA) with very diluted urine.

HPI   The patient drinks several liters of water every day. He was well until this time. The patient also admits to frequent urination (including nocturia) of large volumes of clear, watery urine.

PE   VS: slight tachycardia. PE: mild dryness of mucous membranes; visual field testing normal; no papilledema, pupils equal; remainder of PE unremarkable.

Labs   **Low urine specific gravity** (< 1.006); **low urine osmolarity** (< 200 mOsm/L); **elevated serum osmolality** (> 290 mOsm/L); **hypernatremia;** inability to concentrate urine with fluid restriction (hypernatremia increases and urinary osmolality continues to be low).

Imaging   CT: may show masses or lesions in hypothalamus.

Gross Pathology   N/A

Micro Pathology   N/A

Treatment   Central (primary) diabetes insipidus: intranasal desmopressin. Nephrogenic (secondary) diabetes insipidus: add indomethacin, amiloride, and/or hydrochlorothiazide.

Discussion   Caused by a antidiuretic hormone (ADH) deficiency (= PRIMARY) or by renal unresponsiveness to ADH (= NEPHROGENIC OR SECONDARY). Primary diabetes insipidus is caused by surgical, traumatic, or anoxic damage to the hypothalamus or pituitary stalk during pregnancy **(Sheehan's syndrome).** Deficiency of ADH results in **renal loss of free water and hypernatremia.**

ID/CC A 28-year-old seamstress is admitted to the internal medicine ward because of malaise, **confusion, abdominal pain,** vomiting, and diarrhea.

HPI She is a known insulin-dependent **diabetic** (IDDM type I, juvenile onset). One day before her admission, she went out to celebrate her birthday and drank **alcohol** until she became intoxicated (she also forgot to administer insulin).

PE VS: tachycardia (92); hypotension (BP 90/50) (due to hypovolemia); tachypnea (32) (due to respiratory compensation for metabolic acidosis). PE: **dehydration;** peripheral cyanosis; cold, dry skin; **peculiar fruity breath smell** (due to ketone bodies, acetoacetate, and beta-OH-butyrate).

Labs CBC: leukocytosis (14,000) (without infection). Lytes: hyponatremia (130 mEq/L). ABGs: **markedly reduced bicarbonate** (10 mEq/L); **acidosis** (pH = 7.1). Increased ketones in blood; increased creatinine; **hyperglycemia; increased anion gap** (between 10 and 18) (anion gap is calculated as follows: $[Na + K] - [Cl + HCO_3]$); increased amylase (without pancreatitis). UA: glycosuria; ketonuria.

Imaging N/A

Gross Pathology N/A

Micro Pathology N/A

Treatment Nasogastric tube, correction of fluid deficit (caution due to risk of producing cerebral edema). Potassium. Gradual lowering of glucose with insulin. Prophylactic heparin.

Discussion Ketoacidosis might be the first manifestation of diabetes. It is more common in insulin-dependent diabetics than hyperosmolar coma. Usually follows a period of physical or mental stress (e.g., MI, acute grief) or infection.

ID/CC   A 58-year-old white **female** comes to see her internist because of the development of **polyuria, polydipsia** (due to hyperglycemia), and a **skin eruption** that comes and goes in different parts of her body (= NECROLYTIC MIGRATORY RASH).

HPI   She also complains of increasing intermittent **diarrhea, nausea, vomiting, weight loss,** and occasional weakness and dizziness.

PE   VS: normal. PE: patient well hydrated; marked pallor; **erythematous rash on anterior chest, legs, and arms;** no neck masses; lungs clear to auscultation; heart sounds rhythmic; abdomen soft; no masses; no peritoneal signs; no lymphadenopathy.

Labs   CBC: anemia (Hb 7.4 mg/dL). **Markedly increased serum glucagon** levels; **hyperglycemia.**

Imaging   MR/CT: 2.5-cm enhancing mass in body and tail of pancreas; several liver metastases.

Gross Pathology   N/A

Micro Pathology   N/A

Treatment   Surgical removal. Streptozocin if metastatic; insulin; prophylactic heparin and zinc (for skin rash); octreotide.

Discussion   Pancreatic islet cell neoplasm (= ALPHA CELL) that secretes abnormally high amounts of glucagon with resulting **symptomatic hyperglycemia.** It may also secrete adrenocorticotropic hormone (ACTH) and serotonin. Glucagonomas arise from alpha-two islet cells in the pancreas, and the majority (>70%) are malignant. Glucagonomas may also be associated with multiple endocrine neoplasia (MEN) type I.

ID/CC	A 52-year-old obese white male comes to his family doctor complaining of severe pain in the **first metatarsophalangeal joint** (= PODAGRA) that started on the **night** of an episode of binge **eating** and **drinking.**
HPI	He admits to being an avid **meat** eater and drinks **red wine** every night. His history is significant for removal of **kidney stones** (uric acid stones).
PE	VS: fever (38.2 C). PE: **right metatarsophalangeal joint** red, hot, and swollen; painful to active and passive motion; **tophaceous** deposits in left ear and olecranon bursitis.
Labs	**Elevated serum uric acid.** UA: urate crystals. **Increased erythrocyte sedimentation rate (ESR).** CBC: leukocytosis with neutrophilia.
Imaging	XR: punched-out erosions in right big toe at first MTP joint, producing **"overhanging"** spicules.
Gross Pathology	Tophi are white, soft, nodular masses of urate deposits with calcifications seen mainly in synovial membranes, tendon sheaths, and ear cartilages.
Micro Pathology	Tophi and synovial fluid aspiration show characteristic **birefringent, needle-shaped crystals** of uric acid salts; giant cell formation with neutrophilic infiltration.
Treatment	Colchicine for acute stage; administer hourly until diarrhea appears or pain disappears; combined with aspirin or NSAIDs. Afterward, long-term treatment with allopurinol and/or probenecid.
Discussion	Disorder of purine metabolism with resulting increase in serum uric acid level and deposits in several tissues; 10–20% of cases may develop nephrolithiasis; in late stages, urate deposits in the kidney may lead to chronic pyelonephritis, arteriolar sclerosis, hypertension, and renal failure.

ID/CC   A 36-year-old female visits her family doctor because of anxiety, palpitations, **intolerance to heat,** nervousness with hand **trembling,** and **weight loss** despite a normal appetite.

HPI   She is also concerned about increasing **protrusion of her eyes** (= EXOPHTHALMOS).

PE   VS: **tachycardia;** hypertension (BP 150/80). PE: wide pulse pressure; sweaty palms; warm skin; exophthalmos (produced by enlargement of extraocular muscles); **generalized enlargement of thyroid gland** with bruit (= DIFFUSE GOITER); nodular lesions over anterior aspect of lower legs (= PRETIBIAL MYXEDEMA).

Labs   **Markedly decreased thyroid-stimulating hormone (TSH)** (due to negative feedback of autonomously secreted thyroid hormones); **increased T3, T4, and free T4 index;** positive TSH receptor antibodies as well as antinuclear antibodies; hypercalcemia. CBC: anemia.

Imaging   Nuc: increased radioactive iodine uptake measurement; enlarged gland.

Gross Pathology   Increased vascularity of thyroid gland with symmetrical enlargement.

Micro Pathology   Thyroid gland hypertrophy and hyperplasia; reduced thyroid hormone storage and colloid; infiltrative ophthalmopathy.

Treatment   Antithyroid drugs; radioactive iodine.

Discussion   Also called diffuse toxic goiter; most common cause of hyperthyroidism. Idiopathic in nature but with an autoimmune basis; associated with HLA-B8 and HLA-DR3. LATS, an IgG, is responsible for some manifestations. Signs and symptoms are due to excess circulating thyroid hormone.

ID/CC	A 24-year-old woman is referred to the endocrinologist because of concern over **excessive facial hair** along with hair on her central chest and thighs.
HPI	The patient's **menses are regular**, with an average flow of 3–4 days. She is not taking any drugs.
PE	Hirsutism noted; **no clitoromegaly** present (no evidence of virilization); no abdominal or pelvic mass palpable per abdomen or per vagina; remainderof PE normal.
Labs	**Normal** total **testosterone** levels; **normal DHEAS**; normal urine for 17-ketosteroids.
Imaging	US - Abdomen and Pelvis: both adrenals and ovaries normal.
Gross Pathology	N/A
Micro Pathology	N/A
Treatment	No therapy required.
Discussion	Hirsutism that is disproportionate to the patient's ethnic background and accompanied by normal periods is termed idiopathic. If testosterone and DHEAS levels are normal, the patient can be reassured that the condition is benign. If the onset of hirsutism is pubertal with irregular periods, the possibility of polycystic ovary syndrome exists. Recent-onset hirsutism in an adult female, especially when associated with amenorrhea, requires complete investigation to exclude an adrenal or ovarian tumor.

ID/CC A 55-year-old menopausal female comes to see her internist because of progressive **constipation** and **excessive urination** over the past two months; she also complains of **palpitations** both at rest and during exercise.

HPI She has read "all about" osteoporosis during menopause and is afraid of developing it, so she has been taking **abundant calcium supplements** and vitamin D injections.

PE VS: heart rate 80 with skipped beats heard (= VENTRICULAR EXTRASYSTOLES). PE: lungs clear; no neck masses; thyroid not palpable; no lymphadenopathy; **muscle weakness with hyporeflexia;** abdomen soft, no masses; no abnormal pigmentation; **soft tissue calcification** in skin of arms and legs.

Labs **Markedly increased serum calcium** (12 mg/dL) (always correct calcium level for serum albumin). Phosphorus normal. ABGs: metabolic alkalosis. Increased blood urea nitrogen (BUN). ECG: **short Q-T.**

Imaging N/A

Gross Pathology N/A

Micro Pathology N/A

Treatment Force diuresis with abundant isotonic saline solution and furosemide (to increase sodium and concomitant calcium excretion)

Discussion Hypercalcemia may occur in hyperparathyroidism, milk-alkali syndrome, multiple myeloma, Addison's disease, sarcoidosis, prolonged immobilization, metastatic neoplastic disease (due to increased osteoclastic resorption), and primary neoplastic disease (due to production of a PTH-like substance). Some 50% of serum calcium is bound to albumin; preponderance of the rest is actively reabsorbed in the proximal tubule together with sodium. This reabsorption is decreased with expansion of extracellular fluid volume.

ID/CC A 41-year-old obese female comes to the ER with **severe epigastric pain radiating to the back** accompanied by nausea and vomiting; she had been advised to undergo laparoscopic removal of symptomatic **small gallbladder stones.**

HPI She was admitted to the surgical floor and treated for pancreatitis. On her third day, she developed **numbness of the fingers and around the mouth and tongue as well as painful leg cramps** (= HYPOCALCEMIC TETANY).

PE VS: hypotension; tachycardia; fever. PE: patient dehydrated and in acute distress; bilateral basal hypoventilation; abdomen tender in epi-mesogastrium; hypocalcemic signs present, including abduction and flexion of foot when peroneal nerve is tapped (= POSITIVE PERONEAL SIGN); hyperexcitability while using galvanic current (= ERB'S SIGN); facial spasm on tapping over cheek (= CHVOSTEK'S SIGN); carpal spasm seen with arterial occlusion by blood pressure cuff (= TROUSSEAU'S SIGN).

Labs CBC: marked leukocytosis (17,000) with neutrophilia. **Amylase and lipase markedly elevated** (due to acute pancreatitis). ECG: **Q-T prolongation.**

Imaging KUB: **"colon cutoff sign";** increase in gastrocolic space; **sentinel loop.** CXR: small left pleural effusion.

Gross Pathology Hemorrhagic pancreatitis with edema and areas of gray-white necrosis; intraperitoneal free hemorrhagic fluid; chalky-white fat necrosis (saponification of calcium with lipids).

Micro Pathology N/A

Treatment Treat underlying cause, in this case pancreatitis. IV calcium gluconate.

Discussion N/A

ID/CC   A 73-year-old female complains of **weakness,** painful **muscle cramps, and constipation.**

HPI   She suffer from chronic congestive heart failure (CHF) that has been treated with digoxin and **furosemide.** She was also on oral potassium tablets but has discontinued them because of gastric upset.

PE   VS: irregular pulse (atrial fibrillation); hypertension (BP 145/90); no fever. PE: well hydrated; conjunctiva normal; jugular venous pulse slightly increased, third heart sound heard; mild hepatomegaly and pitting edema of lower legs (all due to CHF); deep tendon **reflexes hypoactive.**

Labs   CBC: normal. Lytes: **hypokalemia.** ECG: flattening of S-T segment and T waves; **prominent U waves.**

Imaging   N/A

Gross Pathology   N/A

Micro Pathology   N/A

Treatment   Potassium-rich foods (chick peas, bananas, papaya); potassium supplement; gastric mucosa protective agents; magnesium supplement (deficiency of magnesium frequently coexists). Potassium-sparing diuretics.

Discussion   Potent diuretics such as furosemide frequently cause excessive renal loss of potassium with symptomatic hypokalemia, which, if severe, may be life-threatening. In patients on digoxin, hypokalemia greatly increases digitalis toxicity.

ID/CC A 48-year-old female who has been **on total parenteral nutrition** for two weeks complains of weakness, **palpitations, tremors, and depression.**

HPI One week ago, she underwent a fifth major abdominal operation due to intestinal fistula and sepsis.

PE VS: **tachycardia;** hypotension. PE: patient looks **confused** and "run down"; agitation with muscular **spasticity and hyperreflexia;** heart sounds disclose skipped beats; mild hypoaeration at lung bases; abdomen with three colostomy bags at site of fistula; no peritoneal irritation; no surgical wound infection.

Labs CBC: neutrophilic leukocytosis. Lytes: **hypomagnesemia** (< 0.8 mmol/L); borderline hypokalemia; low 24-hour urinary magnesium excretion. ECG: **prolonged P-R and Q-T intervals; wide QRS; tall T waves; premature ventricular ectopic contractions.**

Imaging N/A

Gross Pathology N/A

Micro Pathology N/A

Treatment Magnesium supplementation.

Discussion Homeostasis of magnesium is achieved through a balance in intestinal (small bowel) absorption and urinary excretion. Deficiency associated with alcoholism, intestinal malabsorption or diarrhea, inadequate replacement in parenteral nutrition, kwashiorkor and marasmus, prolonged GI suction, intestinal fistula, renal tubular acidosis, and use of drugs such as diuretics or methotrexate.

ID/CC   A 37-year-old white female complains of **nausea, vomiting, and headache** on her first postoperative day; the charge nurse found her having a grand mal seizure.

HPI   She had **elective surgery** for a benign left ovarian cyst. Her medical history discloses no previous illness.

PE   VS: no fever; normal heart rate. PE: patient well hydrated; slight **confusion and lethargy** as well as general **weakness;** slight increase in jugular venous pressure; no bleeding, dehiscence (opening of surgical wound), or infection from surgical wound; no peritoneal signs; significant bilateral lower extremity edema.

Labs   CBC: normal. Lytes: hyponatremia (Na 115). Remainder of routine lab exams normal; normal cortisol (done to exclude possible adrenal insufficiency); serum osmolality < 280.

Imaging   N/A

Gross Pathology   N/A

Micro Pathology   N/A

Treatment   Water restriction with caution to avoid osmotic central pontine myelinolysis syndrome, which can occur while restoring sodium levels too quickly.

Discussion   Hyponatremia is the most common electrolyte disturbance seen in hospitalized patients and is often iatrogenic in nature. In a postoperative setting, the metabolic response to trauma is to increase secretion of antidiuretic hormone (ADH), among other hormones, which, coupled with overzealous IV administration of fluids, may lead to symptomatic hyponatremia.

ID/CC A 48-year-old obese white female who works as a janitor at a car dealership is **brought** to the ER **in a coma** after being found on the floor of her room.

HPI Her husband reveals that she has been having **episodes of early-morning dizziness** associated with **hunger** together with dizziness while walking, adding that these symptoms have disappeared when she ate a meal. He also states that the patient has frequently been **nervous and irritable.**

PE VS: tachycardia (105); normotension. PE: patient comatose; mild skin pallor; **cold, sweaty hands;** no focal neurologic deficits; heart sounds rhythmic; no murmurs; lungs clear; abdomen soft; no masses; peristalsis present.

Labs Normal Hb (14.4 mg/dL); blood urea nitrogen (BUN) and creatinine normal. Lytes: normal. **Hypoglycemia** (blood glucose 38 mg/dL); insulin in normal range (due to inadequate suppression); **elevated plasma immunoreactive C-peptide** (vs. exogenous insulin administration where C-peptide is low).

Imaging CT: 1.5-cm **mass in tail of pancreas.** Nuc: mass takes up octreotide.

Gross Pathology Single adenomatous mass.

Micro Pathology Findings according to type of islet cell involved.

Treatment Immediate IV glucose infusion; surgical resection.

Discussion Most common pancreatic islet cell tumor is beta-cell insulinoma (usually benign). Other types include glucagonomas, somatostatinomas, gastrinomas (= ZOLLINGER–ELLISON SYNDROME), and excessive VIP-secreting tumor (= VERNER–MORRISON SYNDROME). Islet cell tumors may be seen in multiple endocrine neoplasia (MEN) syndromes.

ID/CC An 18-year-old female is brought to a local clinic because she has never had a menstrual period (= PRIMARY AMENORRHEA) and shows a **lack of breast development.**

HPI She has a **cleft lip and palate.** On directed questioning, she reports a diminished sense of smell (= HYPOSMIA).

PE VS: normal. PE: left cleft lip and incomplete unilateral cleft palate; **color blindness** on ophthalmologic exam; marked **hyposmia** on olfactory testing; heart and lung sounds within normal limits; no palpable mass in abdomen and pelvis; **no pubic or axillary hair; no breast tissue.**

Labs CBC/Lytes: normal. Liver function tests normal; **decreased gonadotropin-releasing hormone (GnRH); low follicle-stimulating hormone (FSH) and luteinizing hormone (LH).**

Imaging XR - Skull: normal sella turcica. CT/MR - Brain: normal

Gross Pathology N/A

Micro Pathology N/A

Treatment Gonadotropins.

Discussion A congenital, familial deficiency of GnRH with a resulting decrease in FSH and LH levels, producing an isolated hypogonadotropic hypogonadism; typically associated with agenesis or hypoplasia of olfactory bulbs, producing anosmia or hyposmia (lack of stimulus for GnRH production due to absent olfactory bulb catecholamine synthesis).

ID/CC	A 19-year-old male visits his family physician because he is **embarrassed at having large breasts.**
HPI	He also complains of frequent headaches and **impotence.**
PE	**Tall, eunuchoid** body habitus; mild mental retardation; testes small and firm; breast enlargement (= GYNECOMASTIA); female distribution of hair.
Labs	UA: increased urinary follicle-stimulating hormone (FSH); decreased 17-ketosteroid.
Imaging	XR: delayed physeal closure; short fourth metacarpal.
Gross Pathology	Testicular atrophy.
Micro Pathology	**Testicular fibrosis and hyalinization; lack of spermatogenesis;** Leydig's interstitial cells scarce and have foamy cytoplasmic change; **female sex chromatin bodies** (= BARR BODIES) in cells.
Treatment	Testosterone.
Discussion	Also known as testicular dysgenesis; most common cause of male hypogonadism. Alteration due to the presence of three sex chromosomes (karyotype 47, XXY).

ID/CC	A 2-year-old girl, the daughter of an African immigrant, is admitted to the pediatric ward due to an **increase in abdominal girth** and **failure to thrive.**
HPI	She recently arrived in the U.S. from her home country. She was breast-fed until one year of age, at which time her mother ran out of milk. She is apathetic and irritable and has been having frequent episodes of diarrhea.
PE	**Height and weight in fifth percentile; skin and hair depigmentation;** dry skin; hyperkeratosis on axillae and groin; hepatomegaly and **ascites;** thinning of hair; generalized pitting **edema;** loss of muscle; lethargy.
Labs	CBC: anemia; lymphopenia. Hypoalbuminemia. Lytes: hypokalemia, hypomagnesemia.
Imaging	US/CT: fatty liver. KUB: pancreatic calcification (due to tropical pancreatitis). XR: delayed bone age.
Gross Pathology	Fatty infiltration of liver.
Micro Pathology	Intestinal mucosal atrophy with loss of brush border enzymes; atrophy of pancreatic islet cells; widespread fatty infiltration of liver.
Treatment	Restore acid-base and electrolyte balance; treat infections and gradually initiate high-protein diet with vitamins and minerals.
Discussion	Form of malnutrition caused by **protein deprivation** with **normal total caloric intake.**

ID/CC	A 68-year-old obese male is rushed **unconscious** to the ER after he was found lying on the floor of his office.
HPI	He has classic symptoms of an acute MI.
PE	On admission, he is found to be in an acute state of tissue **hypoperfusion** (= SHOCK) with a barely palpable pulse, hypothermia, and bradycardia. Immediate treatment for cardiac shock is begun.
Labs	ECG: acute anteroseptal myocardial infarction. **Increased serum lactate;** hyperphosphatemia. ABGs: **severe metabolic acidosis** (pH 7.27); bicarbonate 14 mEq/L. **Increased anion gap** (19) with no ketoacids; BUN and creatinine normal.
Imaging	N/A
Gross Pathology	N/A
Micro Pathology	N/A
Treatment	Treat precipitating cause of acidosis; administer bicarbonate.
Discussion	A state of increased levels of lactic acid in blood (= LACTIC ACIDOSIS) may be due to a number of causes, including **shock** and **sepsis** (both of which increase lactic acid production due to hypoxia), methanol poisoning, metformin toxicity, and liver failure (due to failure of lactic acid to be removed from blood by its transformation to glucose). The anion gap is an estimation of the total unmeasured plasma anions such as proteins, organic acids, phosphate, and sulfate. Increased anion gap metabolic acidosis is due to salicylate poisoning, alcohol (e.g., methanol, ethanol, propylene glycol) intoxication, lactic acidosis, acute renal failure, and diabetic ketoacidosis.

ID/CC A 45-year-old **female** is referred to a neurologist for evaluation of **drooping eyelids** (= PTOSIS), **double vision** (= DIPLOPIA), and difficulty chewing.

HPI She has been suffering from **rheumatoid arthritis** for several years. She had an **upper respiratory infection two weeks ago.**

PE VS: normal. PE: **asymmetric bilateral ptosis** (after administration of anticholinesterase edrophonium, ptosis improves dramatically); **weakness of arms** (cannot raise arms) **and thigh muscles** (typically, repeated exercise increases weakness and rest restores strength); no sensory deficits; deep tendon reflexes normal.

Labs Increased acetylcholine receptor antibodies.

Imaging CT - Chest: presence of **thymoma**.

Gross Pathology N/A

Micro Pathology N/A

Treatment Anticholinesterase drugs. Thymectomy.

Discussion Autoimmune disease associated with HLA-DR3; characterized by presence of autoantibodies to acetylcholine receptors and thus by diminished neuromuscular transmission of impulses in the sarcolemma at the neuromuscular junction and weakness of voluntary muscles. Sometimes associated with thymoma.

ID/CC A 56-year-old man who is a known non-insulin-dependent **diabetic** (NIDDM type II, maturity onset) and who has been receiving an oral hypoglycemic agent is brought to the emergency room in a **stuporous state.**

HPI For approximately two weeks, he had been treated for an **upper respiratory infection** with oral antibiotics and bronchodilators.

PE VS: **tachycardia;** hypotension. PE: severe **dehydration** with dry oral mucosa and low urinary volume; patient **semiconscious** and **confused;** pupils react bilaterally and normally to light; evidence of proliferative diabetic retinopathy on funduscopic exam; no focal neurologic deficit found.

Labs CBC: mild leukocytosis (12,600). **Markedly increased blood glucose** (900 mg/dL); **increased serum and urinary osmolality** (> 350 mOsm/kg). Lytes: hypernatremia; mild hypokalemia. ABGs: normal serum bicarbonate (no acidosis). Elevated blood urea nitrogen (BUN) and serum creatinine (suggestive of prerenal azotemia). UA: **glycosuria with no ketonuria.**

Imaging N/A

Gross Pathology N/A

Micro Pathology N/A

Treatment Hypotonic (one-half normal) saline. Insulin infusion (e.g., lower dose than in ketoacidosis). Potassium and phosphate supplement as needed. Prophylactic heparin.

Discussion Hyperosmolar, hyperglycemic nonketotic coma occurs mainly in NIDDM patients and is usually associated with an episode of physical or mental stress; not associated with ketosis or ketoacidosis. Volume depletion is severe (average fluid deficit 25% of total body water).

ID/CC	A 44-year-old male is admitted to the orthopedic department because he sustained a **femoral neck fracture when he fell from a small stool;** the type and magnitude of the fracture are not compatible with the patient's age and impact.
HPI	The patient recently emigrated from Somalia and states that he has been suffering from increasing **leg weakness** and persistent **lower back pain.**
PE	VS: normal. PE: complete right femoral neck fracture; **tenderness of lumbar vertebrae** and pelvic rim on palpation.
Labs	Mild anemia (Hb 10 g/dL). Lytes: normal. **Increased alkaline phosphatase;** decreased levels of vitamin D; **hypocalcemia; hypophosphatemia.**
Imaging	XR - Hip: surgical neck femoral fracture. XR - Lumbar Spine: **collapse of lumbar vertebrae; generalized osteopenia.**
Gross Pathology	N/A
Micro Pathology	Excess osteoid but poor mineralization.
Treatment	Vitamin D, calcium supplements; surgical treatment of fracture, physiotherapy.
Discussion	A poor diet in vitamin D and calcium, **lack of sunlight exposure, intestinal malabsorption, renal insufficiency,** or target organ resistance may lead to osteomalacia in the adult (and to rickets in children), with defective calcification of osteoid.

Pellagra (Vitamin B3 Deficiency)

ID/CC A 45-year-old **alcoholic** Hispanic male who recently underwent a strangulated hernia repair becomes irritable and weak, suffers significant weight loss, and develops a **rash** on his face, his neck, and the dorsum of his hands; he also suffers from **diarrhea** and **altered mental status.**

HPI After his operation (which involved a 5-cm small bowel resection), the patient became torpid and anorexic with lack of proper return of bowel function for about three weeks. His home-country **diet** had been based on **corn** products.

PE Erythematous, nonpruritic, hyperpigmented, scaling rash of face, neck (= CASAL'S NECKLACE), and dorsum of hands; angular stomatitis (= CHEILOSIS) and glossitis; diminished touch and pain sensation in all four extremities; apathy, confusion, and disorientation.

Labs UA: low levels of urinary N-methylnicotinamide.

Imaging N/A

Gross Pathology N/A

Micro Pathology Atrophy and ulceration of gastric and intestinal mucosa; neuronal degeneration and demyelination in posterior columns.

Treatment Oral nicotinamide.

Discussion Vitamin B_3 (= NIACIN) deficiency is commonly seen in alcoholics, less frequently seen in GI disorders or elderly patients. It is usually accompanied by other B vitamin deficiencies. The typical observed triad consists of **dermatitis, dementia, and diarrhea.**

ID/CC A 28-year-old male visits his internist for an evaluation of sudden (= PAROXYSMAL) attacks of **headache, perspiration, and anxiety;** attacks are precipitated by exercise, emotional stress, postural changes and, at times, urination.

HPI **Very high blood pressure** has been recorded at the time of previous paroxysms. The patient has a good appetite but looks cachectic; blood pressure recorded between paroxysms is normal. The patient has no history suggestive of renal disease.

PE VS: **hypertension** (BP 180/120). PE: hypertensive retinopathy changes on funduscopic exam.

Labs **Elevated blood sugar** (due to increased catecholamines). Lytes: normal. UA: increased urinary catecholamine excretion; **increased levels of urinary vanillylmandelic acid (VMA).**

Imaging CT/MR: 5-cm left adrenal mass; very high signal on T2-weighted MR. Nuc: MIBG localizes to tumor and metastases.

Gross Pathology Encapsulated, **dusky-colored,** round tumor mass with compressed adrenal gland remnants at periphery and foci of necrosis and hemorrhage.

Micro Pathology Nests of pleomorphic large cells with basophilic cytoplasm and **chrome-staining granules** in vascular stroma; argentaffin stains positive; membrane-bound secretory granules on electron microscopy.

Treatment Treat hypertensive crises with pharmacologic alpha and beta blockade; resection of tumor.

Discussion Most common tumor of adrenal medulla in adults; symptoms produced by increased production of catecholamines. Of these tumors, 10% are extra-adrenal, 10% bilateral, 10% malignant, 10% familial, 10% occur in children, and 10% calcify. May be associated with MEN III (= MULTIPLE ENDOCRINE NEOPLASIA) syndrome.

ID/CC	A **9-year-old** female is brought to her pediatrician because of **breast enlargement.**
HPI	Her mother also reports **cyclical vaginal bleeding** and the appearance of **pubic and axillary hair** since the age of four; an older cousin developed similar signs and symptoms.
PE	Fully developed breasts; axillary and pubic hair present; normal mental development; height and weight greater than average for her age; no focal neurologic signs.
Labs	**Increased plasma follicle-stimulating hormone (FSH), luteinizing hormone (LH),** and estradiol; pubertal pattern of increased gonadotropins after infusion of gonadotropin-releasing hormone (GnRH).
Imaging	XR: **advanced bone age.** US: ovary enlarged to pubertal size with cyst formation. CT/MR: no pituitary lesion.
Gross Pathology	Ovarian cyst formation (luteal); in idiopathic variety, no structural abnormality found.
Micro Pathology	N/A
Treatment	Medroxyprogesterone acetate, psychiatric support; continuous search for possible cause.
Discussion	Most common cause is idiopathic or constitutional; less common causes include hypothalamic-pituitary tumors (pinealomas, hamartomas, gliomas) or lesions causing gonadotropin-dependent precocious puberty.

ID/CC A 53-year-old white **female** goes to her family doctor for a routine physical and is found to be **hypercalcemic.**

HPI She is asymptomatic except for mild **polyuria.**

PE VS: mild **hypertension.** PE: no neck masses; thyroid not palpable; no lymphadenopathy; lungs clear; heart sounds normal; abdomen soft; no masses.

Labs **Increased serum calcium; phosphorus low; elevated parathyroid hormone (PTH); increased alkaline phosphatase.** UA: increased urinary calcium; elevated urinary cAMP and hydroxyproline levels. ABGs: **hyperchloremic metabolic acidosis.** ECG: **short Q-T.**

Imaging XR: subperiosteal bone resorption; cystic long-bone lesions (= BROWN TUMORS). Nuc: increased bone uptake on bone scan.

Gross Pathology Soft, round, well-encapsulated, yellowish-brown single parathyroid adenoma weighing 2 g.

Micro Pathology Chief cells within adenoma.

Treatment Surgical removal.

Discussion Primary hypersecretion of parathyroid hormone may be caused by adenoma (vast majority of cases), chief-cell hyperplasia, or carcinoma of the parathyroid glands. Commonly asymptomatic and frequently recognized during routine physical exams. When symptomatic, peptic ulcer pain, polyuria, polydipsia, constipation, and pancreatitis may be presenting symptoms. May be associated with multiple endocrine neoplasia (MEN) syndromes I and II.

Pseudohypopara-thyroidism

ID/CC A 5-year-old **boy** is brought to the pediatrician because of intermittent **numbness and leg cramps** together with chronic **constipation** that recurs upon discontinuation of laxatives.

HPI His father is also concerned about the fact that his child is **shorter and lower in weight** than his classmates.

PE **Full, round face;** short neck; flat nasal bridge; right convergence squint and left **cataract; delayed dentition;** positive Chvostek's and Trousseau's signs.

Labs CBC/Lytes: normal. Parathyroid hormone (PTH) levels normal; **hypocalcemia.**

Imaging XR: fourth and fifth metacarpals bilaterally are short; **premature physeal closure;** thickening of cortices with demineralization.

Gross Pathology N/A

Micro Pathology N/A

Treatment Vitamin D and calcium supplementation.

Discussion Also called Seabright–Bantam syndrome; X-linked autosomal-dominant disorder in which there is resistance to PTH action on renal tubule with resulting hypocalcemia. Two types exist according to response of cAMP to PTH.

Renal Tubular Acidosis

ID/CC A 33-year-old woman presents to a clinic with **marked weakness** (due to hypokalemia).

HPI Two years ago, she underwent a ureterolithotomy for **renoureteral stones.**

PE **Generalized muscle weakness;** rapid respirations; heart sound with a few skipped beats (hypokalemia gives rise to severe arrhythmias); diminished intestinal peristalsis; no peritoneal signs.

Labs Lytes: increased urinary potassium excretion (due to insufficient hydrogen ion available, with potassium exchanged for sodium) with resulting **marked hypokalemia** (2.3 mEq/L). ABGs: decreased HCO_3 (due to failure to maintain normal gradient of hydrogen ions in distal renal tubules, with HCO_3 loss); **hyperchloremic metabolic acidosis.** Normal serum calcium; high alkaline phosphatase. UA: urine alkaline; hypercalciuria.

Imaging KUB: radiopaque left kidney stones; medullary renal calcification.

Gross Pathology Nephrocalcinosis.

Micro Pathology N/A

Treatment Bicarbonate; potassium and vitamin D.

Discussion Metabolic acidosis caused by renal tubular defects in transport. Type I: selective deficiency of tubular H^+ secretion (produces typical hyperchloremic-hypokalemic acidosis with normal anion gap). Type II: inability to reabsorb HCO_3 (also hypokalemic). Type III: inability to produce NH_3 due to persistently low glomerular filtration rate (GFR) volumes (normokalemic). Type IV due to primary or drug-induced hypoaldosteronism (hyperkalemic).

ID/CC   A 15-month-old Eskimo boy is brought to the pediatric clinic by his parents because of **delayed dentition, poor growth and development,** and frequent crying, weakness, and **constipation.**

HPI   The infant's diet is deficient in eggs and **dairy products,** and he spends most of his time **indoors** (i.e., he has no exposure to sunlight).

PE   Irritability; poor muscular development and muscle tone; abdominal distention; hypotonia of all muscles; anterior fontanelle open; **softening of occipital and parietal bones with elastic recoil** (= CRANIOTABES); **enlargement of costochondral junctions** (= RACHITIC ROSARY); **bowing of legs; lineal chest depression along diaphragm** (= HARRISON'S GROOVE).

Labs   **Serum calcium normal or slightly low; decreased serum phosphorus;** increased alkaline phosphatase.

Imaging   XR: widening of growth plates; osteopenia of cranial and long bones; irregularity and cupping of distal ends of long bones; pseudofractures in metaphysis (= LOOSER'S LINES).

Gross Pathology   Excess amount of **uncalcified bone** at junction of cartilage; bone stretched and pulled out of shape by gravity; increased osteoid seams; osteopenia; frontal bossing of skull; **pigeon breast deformity.**

Micro Pathology   Defective mineralization of osteoid in epiphysis and diaphysis; widening of growth plate.

Treatment   Increased calcium and vitamin D in diet.

Discussion   Disease of infancy and childhood involving **defective mineralization of osteoid** in bone skeleton and neuromuscular system because of **low vitamin D** or calcium in diet; can also be due to low sunlight exposure (vitamin D conversion in skin) and chronic renal failure (blood urea nitrogen and phosphorus levels are high).

ID/CC	A 9-month-old white girl is brought to the pediatric clinic because of **listlessness and anorexia.**
HPI	She is the daughter of an unemployed **poor** urban couple and has never before seen a pediatrician or taken any medication.
PE	Weakness; pallor; **hyperkeratosis** and **hemorrhagic perifolliculitis** of skin of lower extremities, forearms, and abdomen; purpuric skin rashes; **splinter hemorrhages** of nail beds of hands; tenderness and swelling of distal femur and costochondral junctions; **bleeding gums; petechiae** seen over nasal and oral mucosa.
Labs	CBC: microcytic, hypochromic anemia; leukopenia. Plasma and platelet levels of ascorbic acid low; **increased bleeding time.**
Imaging	XR: subperiosteal hemorrhages; both legs and knees show "ground glass" appearance of bones and epiphyses.
Gross Pathology	Growing bone shows diminished osteoid formation, hemarthrosis, and subperiosteal and periarticular hemorrhage; **defective collagen** (vitamin C hydroxylates proline and lysine); endochondral bone formation ceases (osteoblasts fail to form osteoid); existing trabeculae brittle and susceptible to fracture.
Micro Pathology	N/A
Treatment	Oral ascorbic acid (high doses may produce oxalate and uric acid stones).
Discussion	Vitamin C (= ASCORBIC ACID) deficiency is observed in smokers, oncologic patients, alcoholics, infants, and elderly.

ID/CC   A 20-year-old black female visits her gynecologist because she thinks she might be pregnant in light of a **lack of menses for the past four months.**

HPI   She is a **pentathlon athlete** who is training to compete in her home state's tournament next fall. She is sexually active, uses the "rhythm method" for birth control, **and has never missed a menstrual period.**

PE   No breast enlargement; no softening of cervix (= CHADWICK'S SIGN); no bluish discoloration of cervix (= HEGAR'S SIGN) (both presumptive signs of pregnancy); no abdominal or pelvic masses or palpable uterus.

Labs   Serum and urinary beta-hCG **negative for pregnancy;** serum prolactin and thyroid-stimulating hormone (TSH) normal; **decreased serum follicle-stimulating hormone (FSH);** no withdrawal bleeding after administration of progesterone.

Imaging   XR - Skull: normal sella.

Gross Pathology   N/A

Micro Pathology   N/A

Treatment   Advise patient to either gain enough weight to restore menses or take oral contraceptives to prevent osteoporosis.

Discussion   Most common cause of secondary amenorrhea is pregnancy. Women who are involved in vigorous physical exercise and who lose weight may present with a functional gonadotropin deficit. When body weight falls more than 15% of ideal weight, gonadotropin-releasing hormone (GnRH) secretion from hypothalamus is decreased, producing a secondary amenorrhea. The inhibitory effect of estrogens on bone resorption is also lost, predisposing patients to an increased risk for osteoporosis.

ID/CC   A 61-year-old male smoker presents with headache, weakness, **fatigue,** and **decreased urinary output.**

HPI   He was recently diagnosed with **oat cell carcinoma of the lung.**

PE   Cardiac sounds normal; no murmurs; no arrhythmias; no pitting edema; no hepatomegaly; no jugular plethora (no evidence of cardiac disease); no asterixis, jaundice, spider nevi, or parotid enlargement (no evidence of hepatic disease).

Labs   **Decreased serum sodium** (= HYPONATREMIA); **decreased serum osmolality** (< 280 mOsm/kg); normal or low blood urea nitrogen and serum creatinine; no proteinuria (no renal disease); adrenal and thyroid function tests normal. UA: **urine osmolality markedly increased;** hypernatriuria (urinary sodium > 20 mEq/L). **Diminished blood uric acid level** (= HYPOURICEMIA).

Imaging   N/A

Gross Pathology   N/A

Micro Pathology   N/A

Treatment   Water restriction plus a high-salt diet. Demeclocycline.

Discussion   **Syndrome of inappropriate** (increased) **secretion of antidiuretic hormone (SIADH)** occurs with either increased hypothalamic secretion (e.g., CNS disease, postoperative states) or ectopic secretion (e.g., tumors such as oat cell carcinoma of lung). There may also be increased sensitivity to the effect of ADH (as occurs with chlorpropamide, fluoxetine and carbamazepine).

ID/CC	A 25-year-old female visits her gynecologist because of concern about increasing **facial hair.**
HPI	She has also had intermittent **pelvic pain** as well as **lack of menses** for six months (= SECONDARY AMENORRHEA). For the past four years, she has been unsuccessful in her attempts to conceive a child (= INFERTILITY).
PE	Obesity; increased hair on face, back, and arms (= HIRSUTISM); no acne or frontal balding; normal breast development; no clitoromegaly, external genitalia normal; ovaries enlarged bilaterally on pelvic exam.
Labs	**Increased luteinizing hormone (LH);** low follicle-stimulating hormone (FSH) with high LH:FSH ratio; normal prolactin; **increased plasma testosterone** and androstenedione.
Imaging	US: large 6-cm ovaries, each with multiple 1- to 1.5-cm cysts.
Gross Pathology	Pearly, enlarged ovaries with multiple cysts below capsule.
Micro Pathology	Fibrosis with collagenosis of cysts' cortex; luteinized thecal cells; hyperthecosis; no granulosa cells.
Treatment	Clomiphene, oral contraceptives, surgical wedge resection.
Discussion	Also known as **polycystic ovary syndrome;** characterized by an increase in LH, causing excess androgen production by the ovaries, anovulatory cycles (= loss of midcycle temperature elevation), and multiple ovarian cysts. Associated with increased incidence of endometrial carcinoma (due to peripheral conversion of androgens to estrogens). An androgen-secreting tumor of the ovary may also produce the characteristic **triad of secondary amenorrhea, obesity, and hirsutism.**

ID/CC After a routine pelvic exam, a 23-year-old female is referred by her family physician to an endocrinologist for an evaluation due to **"lack of a palpable cervix."**

HPI The patient states that she **has never had a menstrual period.**

PE **Breast tissue bilaterally; absence of pubic and axillary hair;** vagina ends in blind pouch; small atrophic **testis found** on right inguinal canal.

Labs Normal testosterone level (adult male range). Karyotype: **46, XY.**

Imaging US: uterus and ovaries absent.

Gross Pathology N/A

Micro Pathology N/A

Treatment Treat as woman, resect cryptorchid testis and look for the intra-abdominal one.

Discussion Androgen insensitivity syndrome consists of a genotypically male individual (= KARYOTYPE 46, XY) who presents with a female body habitus with breast development and cryptorchidism due to a Y chromosome gene defect that causes the **testosterone receptor protein to be unresponsive to androgenic stimulation.**

Thyroid Storm (Thyrotoxic Crisis)

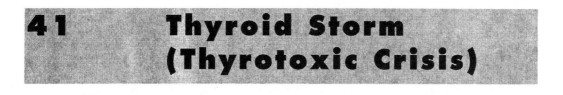

ID/CC   A 29-year-old female is brought by ambulance to the emergency room from her workplace due to **confusion, agitation, and vomiting.**

HPI   Her sister has myasthenia gravis. On directed questioning, she gives a history of **recent weight loss (7 kg)** and a **recent severe upper respiratory infection.**

PE   VS: **fever** (39.3 C); **tachycardia** with irregular pulse; hypotension (BP 100/50). PE: irritability; **delirium;** exophthalmos; diffuse increase in size of thyroid gland (= GOITER); lungs clear; abdomen soft and nontender; no masses; no peritoneal irritation; deep tendon reflexes brisk; no neck stiffness or focal neurologic signs.

Labs   CBC/Lytes: normal. LP: CSF values normal. ECG: atrial fibrillation.

Imaging   N/A

Gross Pathology   N/A

Micro Pathology   N/A

Treatment   Rehydration, antiarrhythmic drugs for atrial fib, **antithyroid agents** (with iodine to prevent hormone release).

Discussion   Thyroid storm, a medical emergency, is usually precipitated by surgical or medical stress (e.g., infection) placed on untreated or undertreated hyperthyroid patient. Prevention of postoperative crises effected through use of iodine and antithyroid drugs.

ID/CC   A 27-year-old Cuban political dissident visits a medical clinic complaining of **diminished visual acuity, primarily at night**.

HPI   He recently arrived in the U.S. by boat after spending several years in prison.

PE   VS: normal. PE: conjunctiva shows diminished tear lubrication with dryness (= XEROSIS; WHEN LOCALIZED, IT FORMS PATCHES KNOWN AS BITOT'S SPOTS) as well as keratinization and small corneal ulcers (= XEROPHTHALMIA).

Labs   N/A

Imaging   N/A

Gross Pathology   N/A

Micro Pathology   Keratinizing metaplasia in conjunctiva and respiratory tract with bronchial dilatation (= BRONCHIECTASIS); follicular hyperkeratosis with glandular plugging.

Treatment   Vitamin A supplementation.

Discussion   Vitamin A (= RETINOL) is a fat-soluble vitamin derived from beta carotenes that is used for the synthesis of rhodopsin in the retina and for wound healing. Night blindness (= NYCTALOPIA) is an early symptom of vitamin A deficiency; conjunctival xerosis and Bitot's spots are early signs.

ID/CC A 47-year-old homeless **alcoholic** man (with a diet deficient in leafy vegetables) comes into the emergency room with weakness, **bleeding** gums, swelling in his right knee due to blood collection (= HEMARTHROSIS), and **bloody vomit** (= HEMATEMESIS).

HPI The patient's diet consists of one meal a day of leftovers from fast-food restaurants. He was given ampicillin for diarrhea two weeks ago (leading to suppression of vitamin K synthesis of colonic bacteria).

PE Patient thin and **malnourished** with poor hygiene; conjunctival and nail bed pallor; subcutaneous ecchymosis in arms and legs; right hemarthrosis.

Labs Anemia (Hb 9.7); prolonged prothrombin time (PT) and partial thromboplastin time (PTT).

Imaging N/A

Gross Pathology N/A

Micro Pathology N/A

Treatment Vitamin K supplementation.

Discussion Coagulation factors II, VII, IX, and X are dependent on vitamin K for their activity (through gamma-carboxylation). Broad-spectrum antibiotic use, malabsorption, and lack of dietary vitamin K result in deficiency, manifested as bleeding. Since these factors are made by the liver, severe liver disease can cause coagulopathy.

ID/CC   A 45-year-old male chess player is brought to the emergency room complaining of acute **nausea**; he has **vomited** five times, feels very **lightheaded**, and has a severe **headache.**

HPI   He went out **drinking** last night to celebrate his victory in a chess tournament he attended last week in Mexico. While in Mexico, he contracted acute amebiasis that is currently being treated with **metronidazole.**

PE   VS: marked tachycardia (120); **hypotension** (BP 90/60). PE: patient anxious, dehydrated, and confused with severe nausea.

Labs   CBC/LFTs: normal. Amylase normal. Lytes: mild hypokalemia (due to vomiting).

Imaging   N/A

Gross Pathology   N/A

Micro Pathology   N/A

Treatment   Supportive, IV fluids, antiemetics, discontinuance of alcohol.

Discussion   Ethanol is degraded by a dehydrogenase to acetaldehyde, which in turn is degraded to acetic acid by another dehydrogenase. This acetaldehyde dehydrogenase is inhibited by disulfiram, resulting in the **accumulation of acetaldehyde,** which produces nausea, vomiting, headache, and hypotension (= ANTABUSE EFFECT). Metronidazole, among other drugs, has an Antabuse-like effect when alcohol is consumed.

ID/CC	A 47-year-old male high school teacher visits his internist because of **chronic watery diarrhea** and **hot flushes while drinking alcohol;** a few months ago he also noticed a peculiar **redness of his face.**
HPI	Every time he works or exercises in the sun, he develops a rash on exposed areas. (= PHOTODERMATITIS).
PE	VS: normal. PE: patient in no acute distress; **redness of face;** no neck masses or increased jugular venous pressure; **systolic ejection murmur grade I/IV at pulmonary area**, increasing with inspiration (= PULMONARY STENOSIS); wheezing heard; abdomen soft and nontender; mild **hepatomegaly.**
Labs	CBC/Lytes: normal. Glucose, urea, creatinine, and liver function tests normal; no ova or parasites in stool. UA: **increased 5-hydroxyindoleacetic acid (5-HIAA) in urine** (a product of serotonin degradation).
Imaging	KUB: ladder-step air-fluid levels. UGI: small bowel loops kinked, causing obstruction. CT: star-like thickening of mesentery due to desmoplastic retraction; vague liver metastatic lesions.
Gross Pathology	Firm, yellow, submucosal nodule in a segment of ileum.
Micro Pathology	Argentophilic cells (= KULCHITSKY CELLS) in the intestinal crypts of Lieberkuhn invading into mesentery; marked fibrotic reaction.
Treatment	Octreotide, cyproheptadine (= SOMATOSTATIN ANALOG).
Discussion	Carcinoid tumors arise from the gastrointestinal tract or bronchi. These tumors secrete serotonin (= 5-HYDROXYTRYPTAMINE), producing the typical clinical syndrome. There may be stenosis of the pulmonic and tricuspid valve and right-sided heart failure.

ID/CC A 3-week-old male is seen by a neonatologist because of **severe jaundice** that appeared at birth and has been worsening ever since.

HPI He is the first-born child of a healthy **Jewish** couple. His mother had an uneventful pregnancy and delivery.

PE Average weight and height for age; in no acute distress; **marked jaundice** (jaundice appears at levels of bilirubin around 2.5–3.0 mg/dL); slight hepatomegaly; PE otherwise normal.

Labs **Markedly increased unconjugated bilirubin (15 mg/dL); very low fecal urobilinogen.**

Imaging N/A

Gross Pathology N/A

Micro Pathology N/A

Treatment Phenobarbital for type II. Prognosis guarded with likelihood of death in first year of life.

Discussion Inherited disorder of bilirubin metabolism; characterized by a **deficiency** of the enzyme **glucuronyl transferase** and hence by an inability to conjugate bilirubin, with accumulation of indirect bilirubin and risk of kernicterus with brain damage (at bilirubin concentrations of more than 20 mg/dL). There are two types: type I, which is more severe and is autosomal recessive, and type II, which is autosomal dominant.

ID/CC	A 21-year-old female college student visits her gastroenterologist for an evaluation of fatigability and intermittent **right upper quadrant and epigastric pain.**
HPI	She asked her family doctor to refer her to a gastroenterologist because she was concerned about her pain despite her doctor's reassurance that it was "nothing important."
PE	VS: normal. PE: mild **jaundice** in conjunctiva and underneath tongue; patient well hydrated and in no acute distress; no hepatosplenomegaly on abdominal exam; no signs of hepatic failure.
Labs	**Increased direct bilirubin** (vs. Gilbert's syndrome, in which hyperbilirubinemia is indirect) **and indirect bilirubin; liver enzymes mildly elevated.** UA: bilirubin and urobilinogen (vs. Gilbert's syndrome); **ratio of coproporphyrin I and coproporphyrin III in urine 5:1** (normal = 1).
Imaging	US: no gallstones; liver normal. Nuc: no biliary excretion on HIDA.
Gross Pathology	**Liver** normal size and **dark green** in color; absence of gallbladder inflammation or stones.
Micro Pathology	Centrolobular, lysosomal granules with brownish pigment (catecholamines).
Treatment	Supportive.
Discussion	A benign, autosomal-recessive disorder (vs. Gilbert's syndrome) of defective canalicular bilirubin excretion characterized by episodes of intermittent jaundice.

ID/CC A 19-year-old male with an upper respiratory tract infection visits his family doctor because he is concerned about **yellowness in his eyes** (= JAUNDICE), which he has noticed **whenever he is fatigued** or is suffering from a minor infection.

HPI He has no history of dark-colored urine, clay-colored stools, abdominal pain, blood transfusions, or drug use. He is immunized against hepatitis B and does not drink alcohol.

PE PE basically **normal except for mild scleral icterus;** no hepatosplenomegaly; no signs of chronic liver failure.

Labs Moderately **increased serum bilirubin, predominantly unconjugated;** normal serum transaminases and alkaline phosphatase; normal serum albumin; **serum bilirubin rises after 24-hr fast.**

Imaging N/A

Gross Pathology N/A

Micro Pathology N/A

Treatment No metabolic treatment available.

Discussion The most common example of idiopathic hyperbilirubinemia is Gilbert's disease, which is inherited as an autosomal-dominant trait with variable penetrance; due to a defect in bilirubin transport from serum to conjugation site or to defective uptake by liver cell. Activity of glucuronyl transferase may be low. Bilirubin levels seldom exceed 5 mg/dL, mainly unconjugated, and may vary inversely with caloric intake.

ID/CC   A 23-year-old white female is brought to the ER because of strange, dreamlike **hallucinations and blurred vision** that she experienced one day **after spending all morning in the sun** painting her house (exposure to paint may precipitate attacks).

HPI   The patient had undergone two **previous laparotomies** for apparent acute abdomen, but **no pathology was found.** She has had several episodes of **recurrent abdominal pain.**

PE   VS: no fever or tachycardia. PE: pupils are of unequal size (= ANISOCORIA); generalized weakness and hypoactive deep-tendon reflexes; disorientation; foot drop; **urine very dark** and foul-smelling.

Labs   UA: increased urine **porphobilinogen** and **gamma-aminolevulinic acid.** Hyponatremia.

Imaging   N/A

Gross Pathology   Liver infiltrated with porphobilinogen, with fibrotic tissue formation (= CIRRHOSIS); central and peripheral nervous system myelin sheath degeneration.

Micro Pathology   Degeneration of myelin sheath.

Treatment   High-carbohydrate diet; glucose; hematin.

Discussion   Autosomal-dominant deficiency in an enzyme of porphyrin metabolism (porphobilinogen deaminase) that leads to systemic symptoms, acute abdominal pain, neuropsychiatric signs and symptoms, and CNS and peripheral neuropathy. Acute intermittent porphyria is differentiated from other porphyrias by its **lack of photosensitive skin lesions.** Sun exposure and drugs (e.g., sulfa, barbiturates) may precipitate attacks.

ID/CC   A 27-year-old **farmer from Florida** (with abundant sun exposure) comes to see his dermatologist for an evaluation of a recent **increase in size** and **change in color** of a **skin lesion** that has been present on the dorsum of his hand (a sun-exposed area) for six years.

HPI   The patient is an **albino,** but he has not been able to comply with his dermatologist's orders to wear long sleeves during work in the field.

PE   **White hair including eyelashes and eyebrows**; eye exam shows **nystagmus** and poor development of macula with red iris and pupil; skin is pink-white with lack of pigmentation throughout body and numerous actinic (SOLAR) keratoses on face and scalp as well as on dorsum of hands; **ulcerated lesion with indurated edges** on dorsum of hand with hyperpigmentation.

Labs   **Tyrosine** assay shows **absence** of the enzyme.

Imaging   N/A

Gross Pathology   Patches of scaly, irregular, hypertrophied skin in sun-exposed areas (actinic keratosis).

Micro Pathology   Biopsy of lesion on dorsum of hand shows epidermoid (squamous cell) cancer with epithelial pearls.

Treatment   Surgery; chemotherapy.

Discussion   Albinism is a hereditary disorder that may be generalized or localized and is transmitted as an autosomal dominant or autosomal recessive trait. It is always distinguished by various degrees of **hypopigmentation** of the skin, hair, iris, and retina. The defect lies in the pigmentation, not in the number of melanocytes present in the body. The cause is an **absence of tyrosinase**, the enzyme that catalyzes the conversion of tyrosine to dihydroxyphenylalanine and melanin. There is a marked increase in the risk of skin cancer.

ID/CC	A 37-year-old man presents with **dark, blackened spots in his sclera and ear cartilage** as well as back pain and restriction of motion with **pain and swelling** of both knee **joints.**
HPI	Directed questioning reveals that his **urine turns black** if left standing.
PE	**Increased pigmentation** in ears, conjunctiva, nasal bridge, neck, and anterior thorax (= OCHRONOSIS); arthritis of spine, both knee joints, and fingers.
Labs	UA: **elevated urine homogentisic acid** (causes urine to darken upon standing or with addition of alkaline substances).
Imaging	XR: calcification in cartilage of knee menisci and wrist; premature arthritic changes.
Gross Pathology	N/A
Micro Pathology	N/A
Treatment	Symptomatic treatment of arthritis.
Discussion	Also called ochronosis; autosomal-recessive disorder of tyrosine metabolism characterized by **absence of homogentisate oxidase** due to a defective gene on chromosome 3 with accumulation of homogentisic acid in cartilage, giving a dark discoloration to the tissues.

Chronic Granulomatous Disease

ID/CC   A 5-year-old male with cough, sputum production, fever, and malaise comes to the pediatric ER, where a diagnosis of possible **staphylococcal pneumonia** is made.

HPI   He has been **admitted to the hospital on five previous occasions** for osteomyelitis, erysipelas, and different pneumonias (with uncommon organisms).

PE   VS: fever (38.5 C); tachycardia; tachypnea. PE: dullness to percussion on right lung; remainder of PE normal.

Labs   CBC: **anemia** of chronic disease. Sputum shows gram-positive bacteria in clumps; later culture confirms staph; **elevated immunoglobulins**.

Imaging   CXR: right lung cavitating lesion.

Gross Pathology   N/A

Micro Pathology   N/A

Treatment   Vancomycin for staphylococcal pneumonia. Treatment of CGD is largely supportive.

Discussion   In CGD, normal phagocytosis of bacteria occurs, but patient cannot form peroxide and consequently hypochlorite as an antibacterial mechanism. CGD is caused by a deficiency in NADPH oxidase, which converts molecular oxygen into superoxide free radicals in neutrophils (= RESPIRATORY BURST); superoxide dismutase then acts on superoxide to produce peroxide, which, combined with chloride via the myeloperoxidase system, forms hypochlorite, a powerful bacteria killer (due to degradation of bacterial wall). Patients with CGD have increased susceptibility to infections caused by *Staphylococcus aureus*, *E. coli*, and *Aspergillus*.

ID/CC   An **11-year-old white** female is brought to the ER by her parents because of fever, **difficulty breathing, and a productive cough with greenish sputum.**

HPI   Her parents are of northern European descent. She has a history of **recurrent upper respiratory tract infections and foul-smelling, diarrheic** stools since infancy.

PE   VS: tachycardia; tachypnea (45). PE: mild cyanosis; malnourishment; **nasal polyps;** hyperresonance to lung percussion with **barrel-shaped chest;** scattered rales; hepatomegaly.

Labs   **High sodium and chloride** concentrations in **sweat** test; *Haemophilus influenzae* and *Staphylococcus aureus* in sputum culture. PFTs: increased RV/TLC ratio. Increased **fecal fat.** ABGs: hypoxemia; hypercapnia.

Imaging   CXR: some dilated bronchi (= BRONCHIECTASIS) filled with mucus; emphysema XR - Paranasal Sinuses: opacification of sinuses.

Gross Pathology   Atrophic pancreas with almost complete disruption of acini and replacement of exocrine pancreas with fibrous tissue and fat; mucous plugging of canaliculi.

Micro Pathology   Inflammatory change.

Treatment   Antibiotics, diet, and supportive measures; recombinant human DNase (cleaves extracellular DNA from neutrophils in sputum), lung transplant.

Discussion   **Autosomal-recessive** disease; due to a mutation in the long arm of chromosome 7 (band q31) in the cystic fibrosis transmembrane conductance regulator (CFTR) gene. If CFTR function is deficient, Cl and water transport is slowed and secretions are inspissated.

ID/CC	A 15-year-old female is brought to the emergency room from school following the sudden development of **severe, intermittent right-flank pain** together with nausea, vomiting, and **blood in her urine** (a picture typical of renoureteral stone).
HPI	Her medical and family history is unremarkable.
PE	VS: tachycardia; normotension; slight fever. PE: short stature (due to lysine deficiency); patient in acute distress; **constantly switches positions in bed** (due to renal colic); abdominal tenderness; no peritoneal irritation; costovertebral angle tenderness.
Labs	**Increased urinary excretion of cysteine, ornithine, arginine, and lysine** on urine amino acid chromatography (due to intestinal and renal defect in reabsorption). UA: hematuria; hexagonal crystals (= CYSTEINE) upon cooling of acidified urine sediment.
Imaging	KUB/IVP/CT Urography: radiopaque stone in area of right kidney.
Gross Pathology	N/A
Micro Pathology	N/A
Treatment	Low methionine diet; increase fluid intake; alkalinize urine; penicillamine.
Discussion	Autosomal-recessive disorder of dibasic amino acid metabolism (due to impaired renal tubular reabsorption); leads to increased cysteine urinary excretion and kidney stone formation.

Duchenne's Muscular Dystrophy

ID/CC   A 4-year-old black male is brought to the pediatric clinic because of **easy fatigability and difficulty walking** of a few months' duration.

HPI   Her mother has noticed that the child's calves have increased in size (pseudohypertrophy).

PE   Child well developed but shows **proximal muscle weakness** in shoulder and pelvic girdle; difficulty standing and walking; "climbs up on himself" to rise from sitting to standing (= GOWERS' SIGN).

Labs   **Creatine kinase (CK), lactic dehydrogenase (LDH), and glucose phosphoisomerase elevated;** myopathy (vs. neuropathic type of disorder).

Imaging   N/A

Gross Pathology   Replacement of normal muscle protein with fibrofatty tissue, giving rise to pseudohypertrophy.

Micro Pathology   Degeneration and atrophy of muscle fibers with ringed fibers surrounding normal tissue.

Treatment   Prognosis is poor, with disability occurring within a few years and death occurring before puberty. Treatment is supportive.

Discussion   An X-linked recessive disorder characterized by a deficiency in muscle dystrophin, a protein that stabilizes actin filaments at the neuromuscular junctions. Course is relentlessly progressive, ending in death from cardiac and respiratory muscle involvement.

ID/CC A 9-year-old boy is brought to the emergency room with pain, inability to move his left shoulder, and flattening of the normal rounded shoulder contour (= SHOULDER DISLOCATION) that occurred when he tried to hit a ball with his bat at a local baseball field.

HPI He has **dislocated his left shoulder nine times before and his right shoulder three times before.** He also has a history of **easy bruising.**

PE **Hyperelastic skin;** "cigarette paper" scars in areas of trauma; **hyperextensibility of joints;** left shoulder dislocated; multiple bruises over skin; blue sclera.

Labs Clotting profile normal.

Imaging XR: left shoulder dislocated.

Gross Pathology N/A

Micro Pathology Collagen fibrils of dermis of skin larger than normal and irregular in outline on electron microscopy.

Treatment Supportive.

Discussion Also known as cutis hyperelastica, faulty collagen synthesis produces 10 types of Ehlers–Danlos syndrome, some of which are autosomal recessive (type VI), others autosomal dominant (type IV) and others associated with X-linked recessive transmission (type IX). Prone to aneurysm and dissection in the great vessels.

ID/CC	A 27-year-old **male** presents with episodes of **painful, burning paresthesias along his palms and soles** along with markedly **diminished vision** in his right eye.
HPI	His maternal **uncle died of chronic renal failure** at the age of 40.
PE	Clusters of **purplish-red, hyperkeratotic lesions** on skin around umbilicus, buttocks, and scrotum (= ANGIOKERATOMAS); **right corneal leukomatous opacity** and retinal edema; neurologic exam normal except for painful paresthesias along arms and soles; pitting edema in lower extremities.
Labs	**Elevated serum creatinine and blood urea nitrogen** (patients usually die of renal failure). UA: proteinuria, broad casts. PBS: leukocytes reveal deficiency of alpha-galactosidase.
Imaging	N/A
Gross Pathology	N/A
Micro Pathology	Lipid deposition in epithelial and endothelial cells of glomeruli and tubules (= FOAM CELLS) on renal biopsy; lysosomal accumulation of glycosphingolipid (ceramide trihexoside) in the form of "myelin bodies" on electron microscopy of skin, heart, kidneys, and CNS.
Treatment	Treat pain crises symptomatically; renal failure may require renal transplantation.
Discussion	Fabry's disease, a sphingolipidosis, is a rare X-linked recessive disorder of glycosphingolipid metabolism caused by a **deficiency of alpha-galactosidase A** and by the consequent accumulation of ceramide trihexoside.

ID/CC A **28-year-old** white male complains of severe **retrosternal pain** radiating down to his left arm and jaw.

HPI He has not had a physical exam in a long time. He adds that his **father died at a young age** of a **myocardial infarction.**

PE Anguished, dyspneic, diaphoretic male with hand clutched to chest (indirect sign of myocardial pain); soft, **elevated plaques on eyelids** (= XANTHELASMAS); arcus senilis; painful **xanthomas** of Achilles **tendons** and patellae.

Labs Elevated CK-MB; elevated troponin T and I. ECG: MI. Extremely **high levels of low-density lipoprotein (LDL).**

Imaging Angio: coronary artery disease.

Gross Pathology Premature atherosclerosis in large arteries.

Micro Pathology Foam cells with lipid characteristic of atherosclerotic plaques.

Treatment Diet, cholesterol-lowering drugs.

Discussion Also called type II hyperlipoproteinemia; autosomal-dominant defect in LDL receptor with a gene frequency of 1:500. Homozygotes have LDL count eight times normal.

ID/CC   A 16-year-old white female complains of sudden **midepigastric pain and nausea** after eating french fries.

HPI   Her history reveals that **she and a sibling** have had similar episodes of abdominal pain in the past. Careful questioning discloses that she experiences **flushing** every time she **drinks alcohol.**

PE   Nonpainful, yellowish papules on face, scalp, elbows, knees, and buttocks (= ERUPTIVE XANTHOMATOSIS); lipemia retinalis on funduscopic exam; hepatosplenomegaly; abdominal muscle guarding and palpable tenderness.

Labs   Elevated serum **amylase** and lipase; **very high triglycerides;** moderate elevation of serum cholesterol and phospholipids.

Imaging   N/A

Gross Pathology   N/A

Micro Pathology   Lipid-laden foam cells.

Treatment   Low-fat diet; avoidance of alcohol, exercise; niacin in selected cases.

Discussion   Autosomal dominant; abdominal pain from **recurrent acute pancreatitis.**

ID/CC A 4-year-old boy is referred to the pediatric clinic for evaluation of **anemia and multiple developmental anomalies.**

HPI His parents report that the child **bleeds easily.**

PE Patient pale and **mentally retarded;** small head (= MICROCEPHALIA); low height and weight for age; hyperpigmentation of torso and thighs with café-au-lait spots; **decrease in size of penis;** decrease in size of eyes (= MICROPHTHALMIA); **absence of both thumbs.**

Labs CBC: decreased WBCs (= LEUKOPENIA), platelets (= THROMBOCYTOPENIA), and RBCs (= ANEMIA) (= PANCYTOPENIA). Increased levels of HbF. Bone marrow chromosomes show diverse alterations (breaks, constrictions, and translocations).

Imaging XR: **bilateral absence of radii.** IVP/CT: **hypoplastic kidneys.**

Gross Pathology N/A

Micro Pathology N/A

Treatment Marrow transplantation.

Discussion Congenital, autosomal-recessive disorder characterized by constitutional aplastic anemia due to **defective DNA repair,** presumably as a result of viral infection; associated with multiple musculoskeletal and visceral anomalies and a higher incidence of leukemia.

ID/CC	A 10-year-old **male** is referred to a genetic evaluation clinic by his pediatrician because of **mental retardation.**
HPI	His mother did not take any drugs during her pregnancy, did not suffer from any major illnesses, was seen by an obstetrician periodically, and was monitored intrapartum. Aside from mild mental retardation, the child has an unremarkable medical history.
PE	Patient well developed physically with grade I mental retardation; **no evidence of** cardiovascular, genitourinary, or hepatic **disease.**
Labs	Patient has been subjected to basic and endocrinologic lab profiles, all of which have yielded normal results. Karyotype: **"fragile gap" at end of the long arm on X chromosome.**
Imaging	N/A
Gross Pathology	N/A
Micro Pathology	N/A
Treatment	Supportive.
Discussion	Second most common cause of mental retardation after Down's syndrome in males (women are carriers); fragile X syndrome should be suspected in any male patient whose mental retardation cannot be explained by other disease processes.

ID/CC	A 2-month-old white male is taken to his family doctor because of lethargy, **feeding difficulties,** and yellowish skin (= JAUNDICE).
HPI	The child has been **vomiting** on and off since birth.
PE	Irritability; **jaundice; cataracts; hepatomegaly;** growth and development in fifth percentile; edema.
Labs	UA: **galactosuria;** aminoaciduria; albuminuria. **Hypoglycemia;** increased alanine transaminase (ALT) and aspartate transaminase (AST); elevated direct bilirubin; prolonged prothrombin time; erythrocyte has **markedly reduced galactose-1-phosphate uridyl transferase activity.**
Imaging	US/CT: fatty enlarged liver.
Gross Pathology	Early hepatomegaly and fatty change with giant cells leading to cirrhosis; gliosis of cerebral cortex, basal ganglia, and dentate nucleus of cerebellum; cataracts.
Micro Pathology	Liver, eyes, and brain most severely affected by deposits of galactose-1-phosphate and galactitol; kidney, heart, and spleen also involved.
Treatment	Limit intake of milk and other galactose- and lactose-containing foods.
Discussion	**Autosomal-recessive** lack of enzyme galactose-1-phosphate uridyl transferase; presence of **cataracts** differentiates this from other causes of jaundice in the newborn.

ID/CC An 11-year-old **Jewish** male presents with weakness, **epistaxis,** and a left hemiabdomen abdominal mass.

HPI He has a history of **bruising easily** and sustaining fractures following minimal trauma.

PE Mental retardation; multiple **purpuric patches;** skin pigmentation; mild hepatomegaly; **massive splenomegaly;** marked pallor; no lymphadenopathy or icterus.

Labs CBC: normocytic, normochromic anemia; thrombocytopenia; low normal WBC count. Liver function tests normal; bone marrow biopsy characteristic; isolated WBCs demonstrate deficient beta-glucosidase.

Imaging XR - Spine: biconcave (H-shaped) vertebral bodies. XR - Knee: Erlenmeyer flask deformity of distal femur; osteopenia. CT/US: enlarged spleen with multiple nodules.

Gross Pathology N/A

Micro Pathology Bone marrow biopsy shows myelophthisis; replaced by Gaucher's cells 20–100 microns in size; characteristic **"wrinkled paper" cytoplasm** due to intracytoplasmic glucocerebroside deposition; periodic acid-Schiff (PAS) stain positive.

Treatment Symptomatic, enzyme replacement with purified placental or recombinant acid beta-glucosidase.

Discussion **Autosomal-recessive** deficiency of **glucocerebrosidase** with accumulation of glucosyl-acylsphingosine in bone marrow, spleen, and liver.

ID/CC	A 5-month-old male is brought to the doctor because of frequent nausea, **vomiting,** night sweats, tremors, and **lethargy.**
HPI	When the patient was exclusively breast fed (i.e., during the initial four months after birth), he was thriving; the **onset of symptoms coincided with** the occasional **addition of fruit juices** to the baby's diet.
PE	Lazy-looking, slightly **jaundiced** baby; mild growth retardation; **hepatomegaly.**
Labs	**Marked hypoglycemia; fructosemia.** UA: fructosuria, urine test for reducing sugar positive; dipstick for glucose negative; fructose tolerance test not advisable (may cause severe hypoglycemia).
Imaging	N/A
Gross Pathology	N/A
Micro Pathology	Liver biopsy reveals **low aldolase B activity** (confirmatory test).
Treatment	Return to breast feeding as sole food; avoidance of fruit juices, fruits, and sweets.
Discussion	Any food containing fructose or sucrose (fructose + glucose), may cause symptoms in patients with fructose intolerance, an autosomal-recessive deficiency of aldolase B (enzyme used to split fructose-1-phosphate into glyceraldehyde and dihydroxyacetone phosphate), resulting in accumulation of fructose-1-phosphate within liver cells; if longstanding, it may lead to cirrhosis. Differential diagnosis is galactosemia.

ID/CC A 9-year-old male is referred to the pediatric clinic because of progressive **mental retardation, diminished visual acuity,** and **bone deformity** in the thorax.

HPI The boy was born in Malaysia and never had any prenatal screening.

PE Child tall and thin with elongated limbs; fine hair; **abnormally long fingers** (= ARACHNODACTYLY); **pectus excavatum; lenticular dislocation** (= ECTOPIA LENTIS); malar flush; high-arched palate; genu valgum; cardiovascular exam normal.

Labs **Increased serum methionine; increased urinary homocystine.**

Imaging XR: generalized **osteoporosis.**

Gross Pathology N/A

Micro Pathology Brain gliosis; fatty liver; arterial fibrotic changes as well as degeneration of zonular ligaments of lens.

Treatment High-dose pyridoxine (cofactor for cystathionine synthetase; effective only in some forms of disease); methionine-restricted diet; cysteine and folate supplements.

Discussion Disturbance of methionine metabolism caused by deficiency of cystathionine synthetase in liver cells with accumulation of homocystine. Major arterial and venous **thromboses** are a constant threat because of vessel wall changes and increased platelet adhesiveness due to the toxicity of homocysteine to the vascular endothelium.

ID/CC	An 11-year-old male is sent to the audiometry clinic by his pediatrician for an evaluation of **deafness.**
HPI	His teachers note that he has not been paying attention at school and that his academic performance has suffered as a result.
PE	**Coarse facies and large tongue;** short stature; **corneas clear** (vs. Hurler's disease); dimpled skin in back of arms and thighs; no gibbus (acute-angle kyphosis) present (vs. Hurler's disease); nonpainful nodular lesions on left scapular area; stiffening of joints; deafness.
Labs	UA: increased urinary heparan sulfate and dermatan sulfate.
Imaging	Metacarpal thickening with tapering at ends.
Gross Pathology	N/A
Micro Pathology	Metachromatic granules (= REILLY BODIES) in bone marrow leukocytes; amniotic fluid culture during pregnancy may detect abnormality.
Treatment	Supportive.
Discussion	Hunter's disease, or type II mucopolysaccharidosis, is an **X-linked recessive disease** (a defect found only in males) and is less severe than Hurler's syndrome (type I). Hunter's disease can be differentiated from Hurler's syndrome in that it features no corneal opacities and either no mental retardation or less severe retardation than that found in Hurler's; however, deafness is present. Caused by a **deficiency of iduronosulfate sulfatase.**

ID/CC A 2-year-old white male is brought to the ophthalmologist for an evaluation of **eye clouding.**

HPI The child has a physical and **mental disability** very similar to that of an older **brother** who is also mentally retarded.

PE **Short stature;** very **coarse, elongated facial features** (= GARGOYLISM); **bilateral corneal opacities** (= CATARACTS); retinal degeneration and papilledema; saddle nose deformity; systolic murmur in second right intercostal space; **enlarged heart and liver;** **kyphoscoliosis** with lumbar gibbus (acute angle kyphosis); stiff, immobile, and contracted large joints.

Labs Chondroitin sulfate B and heparan sulfate in urine; **alpha-1-iduronidase deficiency in WBCs.**

Imaging XR: dolichocephaly; increased diameter of sella turcica; deformation of vertebral bodies with scoliosis and kyphosis.

Gross Pathology Increased mucopolysaccharide (MPS) in heart, eye, connective tissue, CNS, cartilage, heart, and bone.

Micro Pathology Enlarged heart; thickened endocardium; MPS infiltration in intima of coronary arteries; meningeal and neuronal deposits producing hydrocephalus; metachromatic granules in lymphocytes and histiocytes.

Treatment Supportive ophthalmologic, skeletal, and cardiovascular treatment.

Discussion Also known as gargoylism, Hurler's syndrome is the most common mucopolysaccharidosis (= TYPE I); **autosomal-recessive; deficiency of alpha-iduronidase.**

Kartagener's Syndrome

ID/CC	A 25-year-old male visits a fertility clinic as part of an **evaluation of infertility** that he is undergoing with his wife.
HPI	His medical history discloses frequent **sinus infections** (= SINUSITIS) and chronic cough with sputum formation (= BRONCHIECTASIS).
PE	VS: normal. PE: apical impulse felt on fifth **right** intercostal space; all auscultatory foci reversed (= DEXTROCARDIA); liver on left side and spleen on right (= SITUS INVERSUS).
Labs	CBC/Lytes: normal. Semen analysis shows **immotile spermatozoa.**
Imaging	CXR: dextrocardia. KUB: situs inversus.
Gross Pathology	N/A
Micro Pathology	N/A
Treatment	N/A
Discussion	**Autosomal-recessive** disorder characterized by lack of dynein (= ATPASE) arms from microtubules of axonemes in cilia of sinuses and bronchi, rendering them immotile. Sperm are also immotile (due to flagellar lack of dynein). Lack of mucus-clearing action causes frequent infections.

ID/CC	A 5-month-old child is brought to the pediatrician because of **growth retardation** and **difficulty feeding.**
HPI	His parents note that the child has been **irritable** and "stiff" (= SPASTICITY).
PE	VS: normal. PE: patient **underdeveloped** for age; **reflexes hyperactive;** paravertebral muscles and hamstrings tense (= RIGIDITY); maternal milk **sucking weak** and punctuated by periods of regurgitation.
Labs	Basic lab work within normal limits. LP: increased protein in CSF.
Imaging	N/A
Gross Pathology	Axonal and white-matter cerebral, cerebellar, and basal ganglia **demyelination.**
Micro Pathology	Basophilic perivascular multinucleated globoid cells (= MACROPHAGES) with cytoplasmic inclusion bodies consisting of cerebroside.
Treatment	Poor prognosis, with death usually occurring rapidly.
Discussion	Also called **globoid leukodystrophy. Autosomal-recessive,** familial genetic disorder characterized by a deficiency of galactosylceramide beta-galactosidase.

ID/CC A 2-year-old **male** is brought to the pediatrician by his mother because of repeated, **self-mutilating biting of his fingers and lips**; the patient's mother has also noticed abundant, **orange-colored "sand"** (uric acid crystals) **in the child's diapers.**

HPI The mother reports that some months ago the child's urine was red (= HEMATURIA), but she took no action at the time.

PE Patient has poor head control, difficulty walking, and difficulty maintaining an erect, seated position; **choreoathetoid movements,** spasticity, and **hyperreflexia** on neurologic exam.

Labs Hyperuricemia (> 10 mg/dL). UA: crystalluria; microscopic hematuria.

Imaging XR: irregular amputation of several fingers.

Gross Pathology N/A

Micro Pathology N/A

Treatment Allopurinol. Removal of primary teeth.

Discussion X-linked metabolic disease resulting from deficiency of an enzyme of purine metabolism, hypoxanthine-guanine phosphoribosyltransferase (HGPRT). If left untreated, patients develop full-blown gouty arthritis and urate nephropathy as well as subcutaneous tophaceous deposits. Compulsive, uncontrollable destructive behavior is typical of the disorder. Prenatal diagnosis is possible.

ID/CC	A 5-day-old male presents with **seizures**, difficulty feeding, and vomiting; his mother reports a **peculiar, maple-sugar-like odor on his diapers.**
HPI	His mother had an unremarkable full-term vaginal delivery.
PE	VS: no fever. PE: full-term neonate with irregular respirations, **muscular rigidity** (= SPASTICITY), and obtunded sensorium; fundus normal; peculiar odor in urine and sweat; when child's head support (hand) is suddenly withdrawn in supine position, patient fails to react with normal extension-abduction followed by flexion and adduction of arms (= ABSENCE OF MORO REFLEX).
Labs	**Hypoglycemia.** ABGs: metabolic acidosis. **Marked elevation in blood and urine levels of** the branched chain amino acids **leucine, isoleucine, alloisoleucine, and valine** as well as decreased levels of alanine, threonine, and serine.
Imaging	N/A
Gross Pathology	Edema of brain with gliosis and white matter **demyelination.**
Micro Pathology	N/A
Treatment	**Removal of branched-chain amino acids** from diet; peritoneal dialysis; thiamine supplementation.
Discussion	**Autosomal-recessive** branched-chain alpha-ketoacidemia; results from defective oxidative decarboxylation of the branched-chain alpha-ketoacids. This decarboxylation is usually accomplished by a complex enzyme system (alpha-ketodehydrogenase) using thiamine as a coenzyme. Deficiency of this enzyme system causes urine to have characteristic maple syrup odor and causes CNS symptoms in first few weeks of life.

ID/CC A 3-year-old white male is brought to the pediatrician because of **increasing difficulty walking** due to **spasticity.**

HPI The child had been developing normally up to now, and his medical history is unremarkable.

PE **Difficulty climbing stairs; ataxia; wide-based gait;** extensor plantar response and hyperreflexia.

Labs LP: increased protein in CSF (vs. cerebral palsy). Decreased peripheral nerve conduction velocity.

Imaging MR - Brain: demyelination.

Gross Pathology Generalized demyelination (due to deficiency of arylsulfatase A interfering with normal metabolism of myelin lipids).

Micro Pathology Toluidine blue staining shows brownish (= METACHROMATIC) granules in oligodendrocytes and neurons of globus pallidus, thalamus, and dentate nucleus.

Treatment Poor prognosis; patients become invalids within a few years and die before puberty.

Discussion **Autosomal-recessive** disorder of sphingolipid metabolism; due to a **deficiency in the enzyme arylsulfatase A** with accumulation of sulfatides in central and peripheral nervous system as well as in kidneys. Intrauterine diagnosis is possible.

ID/CC	An 11-month-old **Jewish** male of **Ashkenazi** descent presents with globally delayed development and **diminished visual acuity.**
HPI	His parents feel that the baby is not acquiring new skills and that existing ones are regressing. They also feel that their child cannot see or hear properly.
PE	**Lymphadenopathy;** hepatosplenomegaly; **cherry-red spot at macula** on funduscopy; malnourished infant with protuberant abdomen; global developmental delay; hypoacusis.
Labs	CBC: mild normochromic, normocytic anemia.
Imaging	N/A
Gross Pathology	N/A
Micro Pathology	Sphingomyelinase deficiency in cultured skin fibroblasts on bone marrow biopsy; characteristic "foam cells" containing sphingomyelin and cholesterol.
Treatment	No treatment available, poor prognosis with death occurring within a few years of birth.
Discussion	Autosomal-recessive deficiency of sphingomyelinase with accumulation of sphingomyelin in lysosomes of histiocytes in brain, bone marrow, spleen, and liver.

ID/CC   A 2-year-old female is referred to a pediatric clinic for evaluation of **lethargy, weakness, and persistent anemia** that has been unresponsive to treatment with iron, folic acid, and vitamins C and B_{12}.

HPI   She is the third-born child of a healthy white couple; her mother had an uneventful pregnancy and a eutopic delivery. Both brothers are healthy.

PE   **Low weight and height** for age; **marked pallor;** flaccidity and lethargy; **sleepiness.** No focal neurologic signs; lungs clear; heart sound with slight aortic systolic ejection murmur (due to anemia); abdomen soft; no masses; no hepatomegaly; spleen barely palpable; no lymphadenopathy.

Labs   CBC: **megaloblastic anemia;** elevated mean corpuscular volume. UA: increased orotic acid excretion with formation of **orotic acid crystals.**

Imaging   N/A

Gross Pathology   N/A

Micro Pathology   N/A

Treatment   Administration of uridine and cytidine. Steroids.

Discussion   Autosomal-recessive disorder of pyrimidine synthesis; caused by a deficiency of the enzyme system orotidylic pyrophosphorylase-orotidylic decarboxylase with resultant megaloblastic anemia due to impaired synthesis of nucleic acids necessary for hematopoiesis.

ID/CC	A 5-year-old white male is brought to the emergency room with a fracture of his right forearm that he sustained after falling off a couch.
HPI	This is the **fifth bone fracture** that the child has sustained **in the past two years.**
PE	**Bluish sclera;** right leg and right arm slightly deformed from poor healing of past fractures; mild **kyphosis and scoliosis** of thoracic spine; **hypotonia and laxity** of right leg and arm; **partial conduction deafness** in both ears.
Labs	N/A
Imaging	XR: fracture of radius and ulna with evidence of osteopenia.
Gross Pathology	N/A
Micro Pathology	**Marked thinning of bone cortices** (= EGGSHELL CORTEX) and rarefaction of trabeculae (due to abnormal synthesis of type I collagen); abnormal softening of tooth enamel.
Treatment	Supportive.
Discussion	Also called brittle bone disease; autosomal-dominant disorder of connective tissue in which there is deficient ossification due to inadequate osteoid formation.

ID/CC   A 19-year-old **male** comes to see the nurse at the college health department complaining of **abdominal and lumbar pain,** which characteristically occurs **when he takes his multivitamin pills** two times a week (Iron, infections, or vaccination are precipitating factors); he has also noticed **dark brown urine the morning after** he has the pain (due to hemolysis).

HPI   He has just left his parents to go to college and is excited about his newfound freedom; he likes to drink excessive amounts of beer.

PE   Marked **pallor;** lung fields clear to auscultation; heart sounds normal; abdomen soft and nontender with no masses or peritoneal signs; no focal neurologic signs.

Labs   CBC: normocytic, normochromic **hemolytic anemia** with reticulocytosis. **Hemoglobinemia and hemoglobinuria;** sucrose hemolysis test positive; **acidified serum test positive (= HAM'S TEST); decreased haptoglobin; elevated LDH; decreased leukocyte alkaline phosphatase.**

Imaging   CXR/KUB: within normal limits.

Gross Pathology   Hemosiderosis of liver, spleen, and kidney.

Micro Pathology   N/A

Treatment   Steroids, bone marrow transplantation. Avoid iron (increases hemolysis episodes).

Discussion   **Autosomal-recessive** defect of the red blood cell membrane, making erythrocytes unusually sensitive to serum complement (there is also an increased binding of C3b). It is characterized by episodes of hemolysis with hemoglobinuria that occur during sleep because of carbon dioxide retention (which lowers the pH, causing and thus enhancing complement activity; first voided urine in the morning is red-brown).

ID/CC	A 6-year-old male presents with progressive **mental retardation, vomiting,** and **hyperactivity** with purposeless movements.
HPI	The child developed normally for the first 2–3 months. He is fairer than his siblings and, unlike them, has blue eyes. He was born outside the United States and did not undergo any screening for congenital disorders.
PE	Child is **blond with blue eyes, perspires** heavily, and is mentally retarded; has **peculiar** "mousy" **odor; hypertonia** with hyperactive deep tendon reflexes on neurologic exam.
Labs	Guthrie test (bacterial inhibition assay method) positive (due to increased blood phenylalanine levels); increased urinary phenylpyruvic and orth-hydroxyphenylacetic acid; normal concentration of tetrahydrobiopterin.
Imaging	XR: cup-shaped metaphysis of radius and ulna; delayed bone age.
Gross Pathology	N/A
Micro Pathology	N/A
Treatment	Diet formulas low in phenylalanine. **Tyrosine supplementation.**
Discussion	Hereditary disorder caused by a deficiency of the enzyme phenylalanine hydroxylase. Neonatal screening program for detection of PKU is in effect throughout the U.S.

78 Phosphoenolpyruvate Carboxykinase Deficiency

ID/CC A 7-year-old female presents with anxiety, **dizziness, sweating,** and nausea following brief episodes of exercise.

HPI These symptoms are **relieved by eating** and do not occur if the patient is frequently fed small meals.

PE Physical exam unremarkable.

Labs **Hypoglycemia** following brief fasting; alanine fails to increase blood sugar; fructose or glycerol administration restores blood glucose to normal.

Imaging N/A

Gross Pathology N/A

Micro Pathology Liver biopsy for enzyme assays reveals deficiency of phosphoenolpyruvate carboxykinase, an enzyme of gluconeogenesis; **no excess glycogen storage** revealed.

Treatment Frequent small meals to prevent episodes of hypoglycemia.

Discussion Phosphoenolpyruvate carboxykinase (PEPCK) deficiency prevents pyruvate from being converted to phosphoenolpyruvate. This deficiency interferes with gluconeogenesis from three-carbon precursors (e.g., alanine) that enter the gluconeogenetic pathway at or below the pyruvate level.

ID/CC	A two-month-old child is brought to the pediatrician because of **failure to gain weight,** increasing **weakness,** insufficient strength to breast feed, and **lethargy.**
HPI	He is the second-born son of a healthy white couple; his mother's pregnancy and delivery were uneventful.
PE	Mild cyanosis; shallow respirations; increase in size of tongue (= MACROGLOSSIA); moderate hepatomegaly; **significant generalized muscular flaccidity.**
Labs	CBC: normal. Lytes: normal. Glucose, blood urea nitrogen (BUN), creatinine normal. ECG: short P-R; **wide QRS; left axis deviation.**
Imaging	CXR: **extreme cardiomegaly** and congestive heart failure.
Gross Pathology	Significant increase in size and weight of heart (up to five times normal); to lesser extent, hepatomegaly.
Micro Pathology	Extensive intracytoplasmic and lysosomal deposition of glycogen on myocardial fibers as well as in striated muscle fibers, kidney, and liver.
Treatment	Poor prognosis; associated with early death from cardiopulmonary failure.
Discussion	**Type II glycogen storage disease** (generalized); fatal disorder caused by an autosomal-recessive deficiency in the lysosomal enzyme (only glycogenosis with lysosomal involvement) alpha-1,4-glucosidase (= ACID MALTASE), with resulting accumulation of glycogen in heart, muscle, kidney, and liver.

Pyruvate Kinase Deficiency

ID/CC A 5-year-old girl is referred to a hematologist for an evaluation of chronic **anemia that has been unresponsive to nutritional supplementation.**

HPI Both parents are clinically normal and are **first cousins** who are **Amish.** The patient has no history of passage of dark-colored urine or recurrent infections.

PE Low weight and height for age; pallor; mild **jaundice;** spleen barely palpable; liver not enlarged.

Labs CBC/PBS: **anemia; markedly increased reticulocyte count;** peripheral blood reveals macro-ovalocytosis with a few echinocytes; no sickle cells or spherocytes seen. UA: urinary hemosiderin present. Reduced serum haptoglobin; **diminished activity of pyruvate kinase** in RBCs on spectrophotometry.

Imaging N/A

Gross Pathology N/A

Micro Pathology N/A

Treatment Exchange transfusions. Splenectomy.

Discussion Pyruvate kinase deficiency is inherited as an **autosomal-recessive** trait and usually produces mild symptoms (hemolytic anemia); **2,3 diphosphoglycerate accumulates,** shifting the hemoglobin-oxygen dissociation curve to the right (due to reduced affinity of red blood cells for oxygen).

ID/CC	A 6-month-old male is brought to a pediatrician for evaluation of **listlessness,** lethargy, and **fixed gaze.**
HPI	His parents are **Ashkenazi Jews.**
PE	**Excessive extensor startle response to noise** (= HYPERACUSIS); child is sleepy and hypotonic with poor head control and a fixed gaze; appears to have translucent skin; **cherry-red macular spot** found on funduscopic exam.
Labs	N/A
Imaging	N/A
Gross Pathology	Diffuse gliosis; cerebral and macular degeneration; up to 50% increase in brain weight (due to deposition of sphingolipid).
Micro Pathology	Neuronal swelling with cytoplasmic **deposits of gangliosides** (= ZEBRA BODIES).
Treatment	Poor prognosis, patients usually die of pneumonia before reaching age of 2.
Discussion	Autosomal-recessive disorder of sphingolipid metabolism characterized by absence of the enzyme hexosaminidase A, producing excessive storage of ganglioside GM-2 in lysosomes **restricted to the cells of the central nervous system.** Ganglioside GM-2 is a glycosphingolipid with sphingosine, a long-chain basic molecule, as its backbone along with an attached sugar and a terminal N-acetylglucosamine. Prenatal diagnosis can be made at 14th week of pregnancy.

ID/CC   A 7-year-old male is brought to a pediatrician for evaluation of episodes of **fatigue,** restlessness, anxiety, nausea, **lightheadedness,** vomiting, and **sweating.**

HPI   The symptoms appear when he does not eat frequent meals and subside while he is eating. He also has a history of bruising easily.

PE   Patient has **"doll-face" facies;** weight low for age; tendon xanthomas; purpuric patches over skin; **marked hepatomegaly.**

Labs   Lactic acidosis; hyperlipidemia; **marked increase in serum uric acid** (patient may exhibit gout symptoms); **marked hypoglycemia;** prolonged PT (impairment of platelet function); hypertriglyceridemia; IV galactose/fructose not converted to glucose; **hypoglycemia response to subcutaneous epinephrine absent;** normal urinary catecholamines.

Imaging   US: hepatomegaly; kidneys also enlarged bilaterally.

Gross Pathology   Liver and kidneys enlarged (vs. type III glycogen storage disease, or Cori's disease, in which there is no renal involvement).

Micro Pathology   Hepatocytes containing variable-sized **glycogen-lipid droplets** on liver biopsy; nuclear glycogenosis seen; large glycogen deposits in kidney; skeletal and cardiac muscle not involved (vs. type V glycogen storage disease, or McArdle's disease, in which skeletal muscle is involved).

Treatment   Frequent meals to prevent hypoglycemia.

Discussion   Autosomal-recessive glycogen storage disease (type I) resulting from a **deficiency of glucose-6-phosphatase** and accumulation of glycogen in liver and kidneys.

ID/CC   A 19-year-old female is brought to her family doctor by her parents, who have noticed that she has started **behaving oddly;** two days ago they noticed that her **eyes were yellow.**

HPI   She also complains of **tremor of her hands at rest** and some **rigidity** when trying to grasp objects (basal ganglia affectation). The **parents** of the patient are **first cousins.**

PE   Patient shows flapping tremor (= ASTERIXIS) of hands; slit-lamp examination reveals **copper deposits in Descemet's membrane** of the cornea (= KAYSER-FLEISCHER rings); abdominal palpation shows moderate **splenomegaly.**

Labs   CBC: hemolytic anemia (due to oxidative RBC damage by copper). **AST and ALT elevated** as well as alkaline phosphatase and bilirubin, both direct and indirect; **decrease in serum ceruloplasmin** (copper transporting protein); **increased urinary copper** (= HYPERCUPRIURIA); increased urinary uric acid (HYPERURICOSURIA).

Imaging   US: enlargement of liver and spleen.

Gross Pathology   Copper accumulation in liver, brain, and cornea.

Micro Pathology   Liver biopsy shows acute inflammation, increased copper levels, and periportal fibrosis (macronodular cirrhosis); intracytoplasmic **hyaline bodies** (= MALLORY BODIES); degeneration of basal ganglia with cavitation, especially of putamen; and hyperplasia with glial proliferation of the lenticular nuclei.

Treatment   Penicillamine (copper chelating drug), pyridoxine.

Discussion   An **autosomal-recessive** inherited disorder of copper metabolism mapped to chromosome 13 and characterized by increased absorption of copper from the intestine and diminished excretion in the bile with resultant copper deposition primarily in brain and liver. There is an increased risk of hepatocellular carcinoma.

ID/CC A 10-year-old girl is brought by her parents to a dermatologist because of a recent **change in color and increase in size of a warty lesion** on her face.

HPI She has been suffering from **excessive sensitivity to sunlight** and thus does her best to avoid the sun as much as possible.

PE Abundant **freckles** on all sun-exposed areas; **telangiectasis;** areas of redness (= ERYTHEMA) and hypopigmentation; **hyperkeratosis** on face and dorsum of hands; hard, nodular lesion on right cheek; no regional lymphadenopathy.

Labs Basic lab work normal.

Imaging N/A

Gross Pathology Generalized hyperpigmentation with desquamative spots on sun-exposed areas.

Micro Pathology Hyperkeratosis with melanin deposition; **epidermoid carcinoma** on biopsy of cheek lesion.

Treatment Avoidance of sunlight, protection against sunlight. Surgical removal of cancer.

Discussion **Autosomal-recessive** disorder; usually manifested in childhood. Characterized by excessive sensitivity to ultraviolet light; due to **impaired endonuclease excision repair mechanism** of ultraviolet light-damaged DNA in dermal fibroblast. There is a marked tendency to develop skin cancer (epidermoid and basal cell carcinoma).

ID/CC   A 40-year-old woman presents with **weakness** and **easy fatigability** as well as **nausea** and **diarrhea.**

HPI   Further questioning reveals that she has had a long and severe course of rheumatoid arthritis for which she has been taking **methotrexate** (a folic acid antagonist).

PE   VS: normal. PE: **pallor;** mild tongue inflammation (= GLOSSITIS); funduscopic exam normal; chest sounds within normal limits; abdomen shows no hepatosplenomegaly; no lymphadenopathy; **no neurologic signs** (vs. vitamin B_{12} deficiency megaloblastic anemia).

Labs   CBC: **hypersegmented polymorphonuclear leukocytes** (more than 5–7 lobes); **megaloblastic RBCs** (mean corpuscular volume > 100); vitamin B_{12} level normal; folate level in RBCs low (vs. vitamin B_{12} deficiency megaloblastic anemia).

Imaging   N/A

Gross Pathology   N/A

Micro Pathology   N/A

Treatment   Folic acid supplementation.

Discussion   Folic acid is found mainly in green leaves. It is important for the synthesis of DNA and RNA. It also acts as a coenzyme for one-carbon transfer and is involved in methylation reactions. Deficiency associated with alcoholism, pregnancy (= MEGALOBLASTIC ANEMIA OF PREGNANCY), dietary deficiencies, and drugs such as sulfamethoxazole-trimethoprim, methotrexate, phenytoin, and proguanil.

ID/CC A 31-year-old **black male** who works as a Peace Corps volunteer in Ghana visits his medical officer complaining of extreme **weakness and fatigue;** he also complains of a **yellowing of his skin** and **slight fever.**

HPI He recently arrived in Ghana, at which time he was given **chloroquine** as a **prophylaxis for malaria.**

PE VS: tachycardia (95). PE: mild jaundice; circumoral and nail bed **pallor;** no hepatosplenomegaly; remainder of PE normal.

Labs **Elevated indirect bilirubin.** CBC/PBS: **low hemoglobin and hematocrit** (9.3/33) with reticulocytosis (= HEMOLYSIS); **spherocytes** in peripheral blood smear; **Heinz bodies** (precipitated hemoglobin) in RBCs; **low blood levels of G6PD** (diagnostic). UA: hemoglobinuria.

Imaging N/A

Gross Pathology N/A

Micro Pathology N/A

Treatment Withdrawal of offending drug.

Discussion **X-linked recessive** disorder seen in about 15% of American black males. With infections or exposure to certain drugs (e.g., sulfa drugs, antimalarials, nitrofurantoin), patients deficient in G6PD present with a hemolytic anemia due to increased RBC sensitivity to oxidant damage.

ID/CC	A 7-year-old male is brought to the emergency room because of weakness and the **spontaneous appearance** of painful swelling of both knee joints (due to hemarthrosis) as well as black, tarry stools (GI bleeding).
HPI	The child has a **history of prolonged bleeding following minor injuries.** His maternal uncle died of a "bleeding disorder."
PE	Pallor; swollen, erythematous, tender knee joints with blood accumulation in synovial capsule (= HEMARTHROSIS); numerous **bruises** seen at areas of minimal repeated trauma.
Labs	Bleeding time and prothrombin time (PT) normal; **prolonged partial thromboplastin time** (PTT); reduced levels of factor VIII on immunoassay; synovial fluid hemorrhagic.
Imaging	XR: bilateral knee effusions.
Gross Pathology	N/A
Micro Pathology	Synovium may show hyperplasia with hemosiderin in synovial macrophages.
Treatment	Cryoprecipitate containing factor VIII, desmopressin, symptomatic.
Discussion	X-linked recessive disorder (**females carry the disease and males suffer from it**) manifested by bleeding and due to a deficiency in coagulation factor VIII.

ID/CC	A 9-month-old infant is brought to the pediatrician because of **jaundice,** lethargy, and **easy fatigability.**
HPI	The parents of the child are immigrants of **northern European origin.**
PE	Paleness, mild jaundice; palpable **splenomegaly.**
Labs	CBC/PBS: microcytic anemia; small, **rounded,** dark RBCs lacking central pallor; negative Coombs' test. Elevated indirect bilirubin; increased reticulocytes; increased mean corpuscular hemoglobin count (> 35).
Imaging	N/A
Gross Pathology	N/A
Micro Pathology	N/A
Treatment	Folic acid. Splenectomy.
Discussion	A congenital, autosomal-dominant disorder characterized by hemolytic anemia with spherical RBCs and splenomegaly; caused by defect in RBC membrane spectrin with loss of the normal biconcavity and higher rate of splenic sequestration and hemolysis. If left untreated, may give rise to pigment **gallstones** and **cholecystitis.**

Iron-Deficiency Anemia

ID/CC A 1-year-old infant presents at a clinic with **lassitude, poor muscle tone,** and delayed motor development.

HPI The mother is a known IV drug user and has two older children who are in the custody of the state social services department.

PE VS: tachycardia; tachypnea. PE: **pallor**; partial alopecia; ulceration of skin at corners of mouth (= CHEILOSIS); smooth tongue; **nails** break easily and **are spoon shaped** (= KOILONYCHIA).

Labs PBS: abnormally **small and pale RBCs** (= MICROCYTIC, HYPOCHROMIC ANEMIA); RBCs of different sizes (= ANISOCYTOSIS) and different shapes (= POIKILOCYTOSIS). **Decreased serum iron;** increased total iron-binding capacity; **increased transferrin** (due to attempt to transport as much iron as possible); **low serum ferritin** (due to insufficient iron to be stored as ferritin).

Imaging N/A

Gross Pathology Atrophic glossitis.

Micro Pathology Erythroid hyperplasia with **decreased bone marrow iron stores on Prussian blue staining** (vs. anemia secondary to chronic disease, which is characterized by increased iron stores).

Treatment Control cause of iron deficiency; supplemental iron.

Discussion Most common cause is **chronic blood loss,** usually gastrointestinal or gynecologic; secondary to deficiency of iron required for normal hemoglobin synthesis. Differentiate with anemia of chronic disease, in which ferritin is high and transferrin is low.

ID/CC   A newborn male in the normal nursery is noted to be **cyanotic;** the pediatrician is called even though the child does not seem to be in acute distress.

HPI   That morning he had undergone circumcision (a benzocaine ointment was used).

PE   Patient **cyanotic;** lungs clear and well ventilated; heart sounds rhythmic; no murmurs heard; no cardiopulmonary problems evident.

Labs   CBC/Lytes: normal. Platelets, liver function tests, blood urea nitrogen (BUN), and creatinine normal. ABGs: PO_2 **normal. Methemoglobin level 18% total hemoglobin.**

Imaging   CXR: normal

Gross Pathology   N/A

Micro Pathology   N/A

Treatment   Oxygen for acute symptoms. **Methylene blue** (increases activity of methemoglobin reductase).

Discussion   Methemoglobin is an oxidized (= FERRIC) form of hemoglobin that cannot function properly as a carrier of oxygen. Diminished oxygen-carrying capacity that results produces headache, lightheadedness, and dyspnea. Drugs such as dapsone and benzocaine as well as dyes such as anilines oxidize hemoglobin to its ferric form, as do **deficiencies of NADH methemoglobin reductase.** In neonates there is a transient deficiency of this enzyme, and HbF is more susceptible than HbA to oxidation.

ID/CC A 48-year-old white female complains of **weakness, dizziness,** anorexia, nausea, and occasional vomiting over the past three months.

HPI She has also experienced **shortness of breath** (due to diminished oxygen-carrying capacity) as well as **numbness and tingling** in the extremities (due to megaloblastic peripheral neuritis).

PE Slightly icteric eyes; hepatosplenomegaly; smooth, beefy-red tongue (= GLOSSITIS); **loss of balance, vibratory, and position sense** in both lower extremities (due to posterior and lateral column involvement; vs. folic acid deficiency).

Labs CBC: **macrocytic,** hypochromic anemia (MCV > 100); **leukopenia (4,000)** with **hypersegmented neutrophils;** thrombocytopenia. Hyperbilirubinemia (2.5 mg/dL, normal 0.1-1.0 mg/dL); **achlorhydria** (no hydrochloric acid in gastric juice); positive Schilling test; low blood vitamin B_{12} levels; RBC folate normal.

Imaging N/A

Gross Pathology Dorsal and lateral spinal columns are small, with axonal degeneration; flat, atrophic mucosa; loss of rugal folds in stomach; increased red marrow in bone.

Micro Pathology **Megaloblastic** and hypercellular **bone marrow** with erythroid hyperplasia; accumulation of hemosiderin in Kupffer cells; chronic atrophic gastritis.

Treatment Vitamin B_{12}.

Discussion Megaloblastic anemia caused by malabsorption of vitamin B_{12} because of lack of intrinsic factor in gastric juice (intrinsic factor, secreted by parietal cells, is indispensable for vitamin B_{12} absorption). Antibodies against gastric parietal cells are almost invariably present in the adult form of disease.

ID/CC	A 40-year-old male visits his family doctor because of a **chronic, recurrent rash** on his hands, face, and other **sun-exposed areas;** the patient's **urine turns dark brown-black if left standing,** and he has noticed that recurrences coincide with alcohol intake.
HPI	Upon directed questioning, he reports having used **hexachlorobenzene as a pesticide** for some years (a fungicide shown to be associated with porphyria cutanea tarda).
PE	Skin erythema with **vesicles and bullae on sun-exposed areas;** skin at these sites is friable and shows presence of whitish plaques (= "MILIA") (due to photosensitizing effect of uroporphyrin); skin of face also shows hypertrichosis and hyperpigmentation.
Labs	Watson–Schwartz test negative. UA: **markedly elevated urinary uroporphyrin levels; slightly elevated urinary coproporphyrin levels.** Fecal porphyrin normal; **elevated transferrin, serum and hepatic iron;** elevated serum transaminases.
Imaging	N/A
Gross Pathology	Liver shows siderosis, bullae, fibrosis, and inflammatory changes.
Micro Pathology	Skin biopsy demonstrates iron deposits; intense porphyrin fluorescence; and long, thin cytoplasmic inclusions.
Treatment	Repeated phlebotomies; avoidance of sunlight, alcohol, iron, and estrogens.
Discussion	Porphyria cutanea tarda (PCT), in contrast to other hepatic porphyrias, is more common among men than women. PCT is caused by partial loss of activity of **hepatic uroporphyrinogen decarboxylase;** lesions are caused by overproduction and excretion of uroporphyrin.

ID/CC A 38-year-old electrician is rushed to the emergency room after receiving an accidental high-voltage **electric shock** while fixing a power line.

HPI On admission a Foley catheter is inserted, yielding a **reddish-brown urine** (due to myoglobin).

PE VS: tachycardia; normotension. PE: confusion; disorientation; patient complains of **muscle pain** in right arm, leg, and buttock; hand severely swollen and has an oblique-shaped **burn;** "outlet wound" located in right gluteal region and ankle.

Labs **Markedly increased serum BUN** (blood urea nitrogen) **and creatinine** (due to acute tubular necrosis); urea normal. Lytes: **hyperkalemia.** Hyperphosphatemia; hyperuricemia; hypocalcemia (due to calcium binding to necrotic muscle); **increased serum creatine kinase** (due to muscle destruction); **myoglobinuria.**

Imaging N/A

Gross Pathology N/A

Micro Pathology N/A

Treatment Urine alkalinization (with IV bicarbonate); vigorous rehydration (to prevent pigment deposition and acute tubular necrosis); mannitol; prevent further muscle damage from compartment syndromes (evaluate need for fasciotomy). Correct electrolyte abnormalities. Hemodialysis may be required in severe cases.

Discussion Myoglobinuria and reduced renal perfusion from volume depletion may cause acute tubular damage. Other causes of rhabdomyolysis **(destruction of striated muscle)** include crush injuries, heroin overdose, prolonged unconsciousness in one position, arterial occlusion, and seizures.

ID/CC A 19-year-old **black** male visits a family medicine clinic for evaluation of a recurrent, chronic, nonhealing **ulcer on his lower leg.**

HPI The patient has a history of chronic ear infections with discharge as well as **recurrent episodes of abdominal and chest pain.** A maternal cousin is known to suffer from a blood disorder.

PE VS: fever. PE: **pallor;** mild icterus; **splenomegaly;** hypoxic spots with neovascularization (= "SEA FANS") on funduscopic exam; nonhealing chronic ulcer on medial aspect of left lower leg.

Labs CBC/PBS: **sickle-shaped RBCs;** hemolytic anemia. Howell–Jolly bodies and Cabot rings; sickling of RBCs seen on exposure to sodium metabisulfite; serum indirect bilirubin moderately elevated; **electrophoresis shows 85% HbS.** UA: microscopic hematuria.

Imaging XR: various forms of bone infarction, such as collapse of femoral head or H-shaped vertebra.

Gross Pathology Retinal infarcts; papillary renal necrosis; splenomegaly with multiple infarcts; fatty replacement of marrow.

Micro Pathology Hemosiderin in Kupffer's cells with centrolobular necrosis and fibrosis.

Treatment Local therapy for leg ulcer, laser therapy for proliferative retinopathy, antibiotic prophylaxis against capsulated bacteria, hydroxyurea may help increase fetal hemoglobin levels.

Discussion Autosomal-recessive hemoglobinopathy due to a DNA mutation on the gene coding for the beta chain of hemoglobin (glutamic acid is substituted by valine at position 6). Incidence of about 1:400 in African Americans. May present with acute painful (vaso-occlusive) crises or aplastic crises associated with infections.

ID/CC	A 2-year-old male is brought to the pediatric clinic due to marked **pallor, failure to thrive,** and delayed developmental motor milestones.
HPI	The child is a descendant of **Greek immigrants.** Several of his close relatives are known to suffer from a "blood disease."
PE	Marked **pallor; mild icterus;** frontal protuberance and **maxillary hypertrophy** (= "CHIPMUNK FACIES"); splenomegaly.
Labs	CBC/PBS: **microcytic, hypochromic anemia (7.0) with anisopoikilocytosis;** decreased reticulocyte count (due to ineffective erythropoiesis); **target cells and acanthocytes;** HbA absent on hemoglobin electrophoresis; HbF comprises 95%; moderately increased, unconjugated bilirubin.
Imaging	XR-Skull: marrow overgrowth in maxilla; widening of diploic spaces with "hair on end " appearance caused by vertical trabeculae.
Gross Pathology	N/A
Micro Pathology	Increased red marrow; decreased yellow marrow; marked erythroid hyperplasia in marrow-ineffective erythropoiesis.
Treatment	Blood transfusions, folic acid, iron chelation therapy, bone marrow transplantation.
Discussion	Beta-thalassemia (common in people of Mediterranean and Asiatic origin) results from decreased synthesis of beta-globin chains due to errors in transcription/ translation of mRNA (increased formation of HbA2 and HbF). Alpha-thalassemia results from decreased synthesis of alpha globin chains due to deletion of one to four alpha gene loci (the more deletions, the more severe the symptoms). Homozygous patients develop thalassemia major, a life-threatening form, whereas heterozygous patients develop thalassemia minor, a lesser form.

ID/CC A 10-year-old male is brought by his parents to the pediatrician for evaluation of **easy bruising** and repeated episodes of **nosebleed** (epistaxis), usually without any precipitating factor.

HPI The patient states that he also **bleeds while brushing his teeth** and that even a small wound takes a long time to stop bleeding.

PE A few scattered subcutaneous **ecchymoses**; easy gingival bleeding when gums are touched with a tongue depressor.

Labs **Bleeding time increased**; PTT prolonged moderately; **factor VIII antigen decreased** (differentiate from hemophilia A); platelets normal; **platelets not aggregated by ristocetin** (vs. Glanzmann's disease).

Imaging N/A

Gross Pathology N/A

Micro Pathology N/A

Treatment Avoid drugs such as aspirin and NSAIDs; desmopressin acetate (releases von Willebrand factor from endothelial cells); tranexamic acid; cryoprecipitate.

Discussion Also known as vascular hemophilia, von Willebrand's disease is the most common congenital anomaly of hemostasis. It is seen in both sexes and is caused by a deficiency of von Willebrand factor. There are three types. Types I and II are the most common and inherited as an autosomal dominant trait; Type III is rare and autosomal recessive. Characterized by mucosal, GI, and dental bleeding; bleeding typically increases with aspirin and decreases with pregnancy and estrogens. No spontaneous hemarthroses are seen (vs. hemophilia A).

Acute Respiratory Distress Syndrome (ARDS)

ID/CC   A 27-year-old medical student is rushed to the emergency room by his classmates because of protracted **vomiting that caused bronchial aspiration.**

HPI   He had been partying for two days and had been **drinking alcohol and smoking marijuana** (clouded sensorium, cough reflex diminished).

PE   Twelve hours after admission, he had to be transferred to ICU because of severe respiratory distress with **cyanosis,** dyspnea, **tachypnea,** intercostal and supraclavicular retractions, rales, wheezing and rhonchi throughout, and shock.

Labs   Profound hypoxemia unresponsive to treatment (= SHUNTING). ABGs: respiratory alkalosis; **increased alveolar-arterial gradient.**

Imaging   CXR: diffuse alveolar densities characteristically sparing costophrenic angle; air bronchogram (= PERIBRONCHIOLAR EDEMA).

Gross Pathology   Severe pulmonary edema with hyaline fibrinous membrane formation.

Micro Pathology   N/A

Treatment   Mechanical ventilation, ICU care, antibiotics if septic complications ensue.

Discussion   ARDS may be due to sepsis, aspiration, trauma-burns, or drug overdosage. After the insult, neutrophils release proteases, free radicals, and leukotrienes, and the lymphocytes and macrophages release interleukin-1 and tumor necrosis factor, all of which cause vasoconstriction and increase vascular permeability with protein leakage into alveoli. Surfactant production is decreased, resulting in widespread atelectasis, intrapulmonary shunting, and hypoxemia.

ID/CC A 36-year-old female **nonsmoker** visits her family doctor because she has become increasingly **short of breath** (= DYSPNEA); her symptoms once appeared only during exercise but now occur even when she is at rest.

HPI She also complains of frequent upper respiratory infections and moderate **weight loss.**

PE **Thin** female with **increased anteroposterior diameter of chest** (= BARREL-SHAPED CHEST); decreased breath sounds bilaterally; **hyperresonance** to percussion; retardation of expiratory flow.

Labs CBC: increased hematocrit. PFTs: **FEV_1/FVC less than 75%** (diagnostic of airflow obstruction). ECG: right ventricular hypertrophy.

Imaging CXR: hyperlucent lung fields; flattening of diaphragm and decreased lung markings at periphery.

Gross Pathology Destruction of alveolar walls distal to the terminal bronchiole with hyperaeration (= EMPHYSEMA); **panacinar type** (= COTTON CANDY LUNG); more severe at lung bases.

Micro Pathology N/A

Treatment Standard treatment for chronic obstructive pulmonary disease (COPD) patients.

Discussion Pollutants, cigarette smoke, and infections increase polymorphonuclear leukocytes (PMNs) and macrophages in the lung and thus produce a number of proteolytic enzymes. Damage to lung tissue due to these enzymes is controlled by the globulin alpha-1-antitrypsin, which inhibits trypsin, elastase, and collagenase. A deficiency of this enzyme causes excessive lung tissue destruction and **panacinar emphysema** (cigarette smoking is associated with centrilobular type).

ID/CC   A 23-year-old female college student is brought to the emergency room because of **numbness** of her face and feet together with a **sensation of suffocation** and **stiff twisting of the hands** (= CARPOPEDAL SPASM); these symptoms arose following an argument with her boyfriend.

HPI   A friend reports that the patient has a **history of anxiety-induced colitis, gastritis, and migraine.**

PE   VS: **marked tachypnea** (40); tachycardia (90); hypertension (BP 140/90). PE: patient **apprehensive** and anxious; physical exam otherwise normal.

Labs   ABGs: **low PCO_2; respiratory alkalosis** (cause of tetany); **low bicarbonate** (to compensate for primary lowering of PCO_2).

Imaging   CXR: normal

Gross Pathology   N/A

Micro Pathology   N/A

Treatment   Have patient breathe in and out of a bag or give 5% CO_2 mixture.

Discussion   Common occurrence in ERs. Anxiety state produces an increase in the frequency of respirations (= HYPERVENTILATION), causing a lowering of PCO_2; resulting respiratory alkalosis produces an unstable depolarization of distal segments of motor nerves with symptomatic tetany. Alkalosis sets in motion a compensatory increase in bicarbonate level to maintain pH as close to normal as possible.

ID/CC A 36-year-old divorcee living in rural Maine is brought by ambulance to the ER with her two children, who were **all found unconscious in her home** by military personnel.

HPI A recent "El Niño" produced bad weather that resulted in a power failure; as a result, she had been using charcoal and a **wooden stove inside her house** for heating purposes.

PE **Skin bright red** (= CHERRY RED CYANOSIS); pulse arrhythmic; patient regains consciousness soon after administration of 100% oxygen but remains drowsy, **disoriented,** and nauseous and complains of a severe **headache** (due to cerebral edema); **hyperreflexia** noted as well as positive Romberg's test.

Labs **Increased carboxyhemoglobin** (>25%). ABGs: metabolic acidosis.

Imaging CT/MR: bilateral globus pallidus lesions.

Gross Pathology N/A

Micro Pathology N/A

Treatment 100% **oxygen,** assisted ventilation if necessary. Hyperbaric oxygen chamber.

Discussion Common sources of CO are car exhaust, pipes, and fires. Carbon monoxide has a much greater affinity for hemoglobin than oxygen (250 times more). If patient is pregnant, damage to fetus is devastating (HbF has more affinity to CO than HbA). Long-term side effects such as memory problems, lack of coordination, and even convulsions are not uncommon after intoxication.

ID/CC	A **premature** (32-week-old) male infant is brought to the intensive care unit after a **cesarean.**
HPI	His mother had third-trimester **bleeding** and contractions that did not stop with rest and conservative treatment.
PE	VS: tachypnea. PE: child weighs 3.8 lb; **cyanosis; dyspnea;** uses accessory muscles of respiration; **nasal flaring.**
Labs	ABGs: hypoxemia; hypercapnia. Decreased lecithin/sphingomyelin (L/S) ratio (L/S ratio normally > 2; 1.5—2.0 in 40% of newborns with RDS).
Imaging	CXR: **reticular pulmonary infiltrates** bilaterally and atelectasis.
Gross Pathology	Generalized atelectasis in purple-colored lung; eosinophilic fibrinous hyaline membrane formation.
Micro Pathology	N/A
Treatment	Ventilatory support, fluid, acid-base and electrolyte balance, antibiotics.
Discussion	**Idiopathic respiratory distress syndrome** of the newborn is the most common cause of death in premature infants. It is due to a **deficiency of surfactant,** a lipoprotein produced by pneumocyte II cells that has detergent effects on alveolar superficial tension and contains the phospholipid dipalmitoyl lecithin. Fetal lung maturity may be measured by the L/S ratio (lecithin to sphingomyelin). The syndrome might be prevented by giving **betamethasone** to pregnant women, since pneumocyte II differentiation is dependent on steroids.

About the Authors

VIKAS BHUSHAN, MD
Vikas is a diagnostic radiologist in Los Angeles and the series editor for *Underground Clinical Vignettes*. His interests include traveling, reading, writing, and world music. He is single and can be reached at vbhushan@aol.com.

CHIRAG AMIN, MD
Chirag is an orthopedics resident at Orlando Regional Medical Center. He can be reached at chiragamin@aol.com.

TAO LE, MD
Tao is completing a medicine residency at Yale-New Haven Hospital and is applying for a fellowship in allergy and immunology. He is married to Thao, who is a pediatrics resident. He can be reached at taotle@aol.com.

JOSE M. FIERRO, MD
Jose (Pepe) is beginning a med/peds residency at Brookdale University Hospital in New York. He is a general surgeon from Mexico who worked extensively in Central Africa. His interests include world citizenship and ethnic music. He is married and can be reached at fierro@mail.dsinet.com.mx.

VISHAL PALL, MBBS
Vishal recently completed medical school and internship in Chandigarh, India. He hopes to begin his residency training in the US in July 1999. He can be reached at mona@puniv.chd.nic.in.

HOANG NGUYEN
Hoang (Henry) is a third-year MD/PhD student at Northwestern University. Henry is single and lives in Chicago, where he spends his free time writing, reading, and enjoying music. He can be reached at hbnguyen@nwu.edu.